THE NEOCOMMUNIST MANIFESTO

THE
NEOCOMMUNIST
MANIFESTO

Filip Spagnoli

Algora Publishing
New York

Library of Congress Cataloging-in-Publication Data —

Spagnoli, Filip.
  The neo-communist manifesto / Filip Spagnoli.
      p. cm.
  Includes bibliographical references and index.
      ISBN 978-0-87586-735-9 (trade paper: alk. paper) — ISBN
978-0-87586-736-6 (case laminate: alk. paper) 1. Communism. 2.
Communism—History—21st century. I. Title.
      HX45.S67 2010
      335.43—dc22
                                    2009037623

Front cover:

Printed in the United States

TABLE OF CONTENTS

INTRODUCTION   1

CHAPTER 1. POLITICS AND THE ECONOMY   7

The Priority of the Economy   7

Ideology   10

Religion   10

Different Kinds of Rule   12

Substructure and Superstructure   14

Substructure and Human Rights   16

Substructure and the Mind   18

Evolving Politics   21

Power and Ownership of the Means of Production   23

The Mind and the Futility of Individuality   24

CHAPTER 2. TO THE REALM OF FREEDOM   31

Dogmatic Optimism and Utopian Fatalism   31

Communist Science   32

History and Post-History   34

Exploitation and Surplus Value   35

The Price for the Regeneration of Labor Power   38

Intensification of the Class Struggle   41

Labor, Nature, Freedom   43

Labor and Wage   46
New Labor (1)   48
Division of Labor   50
New Labor (2)   54
CHAPTER 3. AUTONOMOUS DEVELOPMENT   59
Historical materialism   59
Between the Imposed and the Fabricated   62
Community Destroys Capitalism   63
Big Industry Destroys Private Property   66
Preconditions for Communism   68
The Solution is in the Problem   69
The Revolution as Explosion   70
CHAPTER 4. HUMAN INTERVENTION   73
Helping the Inevitable   73
The Dictatorship of the Proletariat   75
Freedom and Necessity   79
Life and Death   81
Russia and China   83
Legality   85
Order Without a State   88
International Communism   89
CHAPTER 5. EVALUATION   91
Control Over Production, Property   91
Power, Democracy and Human Rights   100
Real and Formal Equality   106
Human Rights and Egoism   111
Individuality, Thinking   117
History, Science, Utopianism   120
Wage, Profit, Corporate Social Responsibility   123

Table of Contents

Production   128

Cooperation and Excellence   130

Communist Politics   133

CONCLUSION: THE IMPORTANCE OF WORK   137

REFERENCES   141

Introduction

Some questions to start with. Is the metaphor of the dust heap of history correct and is the demise of communist states (or their transformation into hyper-capitalist ones) the ultimate proof of the inadequacy of the communist worldview? Is communism today no more than the private insanity of a few Peruvian and Nepalese extremists and the hypocritical sugar-coating of the Chinese government's practice of extreme capitalist exploitation? And is the study of the communist worldview useful only for a better understanding of 20th century history and of some of the worst disasters that occurred during that century and that were inspired by this worldview? Or does communism, against all odds, still have something interesting to say to us today? Can it be useful for making the future as well as understanding the past?

The way in which these questions are framed already gives an indication of the kinds of answers this book will try to defend. I think the time has come to admit that the simultaneous rejection of communist states and communist theory, culminating just after the fall of the Berlin Wall and the implosion of the USSR but already apparent at the time when the atrocities of these states first became known, was an example of intellectual laziness.

True, one should not separate theory from practice. Many of the errors and crimes of communist states were caused, at least in part, by flaws in communist theory. But communist states did not simply implement communist theory. Their failings were to a certain extent caused by other elements, e.g., extreme interpretations of the theory, economic and social circumstances, inclinations and personalities of communist leaders, etc. Not everything that went wrong in communist states should discredit the theory. Parts of this theory do not necessarily or automatically incite crime and error but remain very relevant and useful to us today. The purpose of this book is to identify those elements.

Communist theory indeed contains elements, core elements, that make its integral implementation impossible and undesirable. And anyway, life or society can and should never be the simple implementation of a theory. Society isn't a piece of carpentry, crafted out of raw materials and according to a plan. In fact it is likely that the biggest mistake or even crime of communist states was their belief that society is a construct. Like carpenters, they went ahead with the construction of a new society, and in order to do so, they had to use force on their raw materials, i.e., human beings.

When you believe that society should be constructed according to a plan, politics cannot be democratic. It has to be in the hands of experts who know the plan and the best ways to implement it. Centralized planning of the economy and all other sections of society has proven to be dictatorial and ultimately catastrophic for communist societies.[1]

---

1 See also H. Arendt, *Condition de l'homme moderne*, Calmann-Lévy, Paris, 1983, passim.

But at the same time every honest and unprejudiced reader should admit that parts of communism deserve to be rescued and that is the purpose of book. This, however, requires a substantial rethinking of communism, a drafting of a kind of neo-communism in which everything that is impossible and/or undesirable is deleted. What remains will not constitute a closed theory, a complete worldview or a blueprint for society — as the original communist theory was claimed to be — but a loose collection of ideas and recommendations. And it will no longer be a scientific description of social and historical laws; merely a set of opinions on social life and proposals for reform.

With this purpose of rescuing parts of communism in mind, I will start by trying to give a description of the worldview of communism, but of communism in a simplified sense because I assimilate communism to Marxism and to the teachings of his most orthodox followers. I do not intend to analyze the sometimes subtle differences between Marx and Engels, nor do I plan to study the way in which their followers have or have not transformed or respected the original theory. Leninism, Trotskyism, Maoism, etc. are, somewhat simplistically, considered as minor variations of the main theme. This is certainly incorrect, but necessary for a concise first step in bringing communism up to date.

However, within these confines, I will try to give an account of communism that is fair and complete and that would have allowed Marx or any other "orthodox" communist to recognize him- or herself, warts and all.

A description is of course not enough to frame a neo-communist theory. The descriptive part is followed by a final chapter in which I evaluate the theory in the light of the historical experience in communist states, current needs and my own convictions. What has to be rejected and what continues to be useful or even necessary? The latter will constitute the core of a new, purified communist manifesto. (Those readers who already have a thorough understanding of communist and Marxist theory can safely skip the first chapters and go straight to the last one).

Some have jokingly called this approach "supermarket Marxism": one chooses from the shelves what takes one's fancy. But why not? Saving what's worth saving is better than either orthodoxy or the dustbin of history.

Of course, neo-communism or neo-Marxism isn't anything new in itself. Since the horrors of "actually existing socialism" have come to light, people have attempted to purify communist theory. Some, calling themselves post-communists or post-Marxists no longer believe the supermarket building is standing upright, but see some useful remnants in the rubble. Whatever the metaphor, the important thing is to save what is worth saving, and I believe that I can offer a new review of communism.

This "choice-approach" implies that communism will not or no longer be the sole worldview, providing an overall view of society or offering answers to all important questions of life. What we take from communism, we put together with what we take from elsewhere.

In the same vein, the word "manifesto" should not be understood in the British sense of the policy program of a political party, because such a program typically offers a worldview. The goal is not to create new neo-communist political parties proposing a coherent and all-encompassing ideology. The improvements in social life, proposed in this book, are piecemeal and can be promoted and implemented by any existing political party, left or right, without any inconsistency.

All this may sound a bit too post-modern and post-ideological, but whatever the merits and faults of post-modern-ism, the two things I've always liked about it are its rejection of all-encompassing theories and its eclecticism. I really do believe that even conservatives and extreme anti-communists can realistically and coherently adopt many of the communist ideas that I try to rescue from the dustbin of history. After all, there's also a conservative anti-capitalist tradition. When I tell you in advance that I will focus on the communist ideas about work, production and self-development and will try to redirect communism towards more respect for human rights — including property rights — and democracy — including corporate democracy — then all this may no longer seem as far-fetched as it sounds.

CHAPTER 1. POLITICS AND THE ECONOMY

The Priority of the Economy

The word "communism" refers to three different things:

- A theory about society and its different stages of evolution.

- A political movement with the goal of bringing about a new, perfected and final form of society as it is described in the theory.

- And a form of government as it emerged and largely disappeared in several countries throughout the 20th century.

I will focus on the first. Communism as a political movement will only be discussed from the point of view of communist theory: what does this theory require from a communist political movement? The different communist political movements and governments as historical phenomena will be absent from this book.

Notwithstanding the strong political focus, communism does not regard politics as a very noble activity. Before the communist revolution and the creation of communist society, the state is no more than an oppressive structure in the hands of the ruling economic class. The nature of the state or the form of government is irrelevant. Even a democracy is an instrument to enforce the status quo of economic class rule. In the era of communism, the state will disappear because there will no longer be economic classes in need of tools to repress other classes. During the transition period of the communist revolution, which is necessary to create a communist society, the state is merely a means to bring about communism and therefore also its own demise. But at that time as well, the state is something negative: a necessary evil used by the new ruling class — the proletariat — to suppress resistance to change.

The economy in general and class rule as a particular economic fact are central to the communist description of the pre-communist world. The economy, the means of production, the labor conditions and the labor relations (which are class relations because society is divided into classes that own and classes that don't own means of production) tend to explain everything else in the world and are a kind of substructure that determines the political superstructure, law, religion and even thinking.

The economy is also the driving force behind the historical transformations of society. Changes in the modes of production, the means of production and class relationships bring about new forms of society, every new form being a step forward compared to the previous ones.

Communist theory teaches that, one day, the economy will automatically and inevitably produce humanity's final and perfect form of society, i.e., communism, a new world, a utopian world of freedom in which we will be liberated from class rule and even from the joke of the economy as such. Our current economic activity, the scientific and technical progress that it promotes, and the class contradictions inherent in this activity, will with absolute certainty put an end to the world of necessity and oppression.

Communism is an analysis of the real world coupled to a prediction of the future world. The prediction is believed to result from the analysis, or, more clearly, from an extrapolation of the evolution which this analysis is supposed to uncover. An important characteristic of communist theory is the belief that there is a grand historical movement, a progression towards ever more perfect forms of society, and that this movement is inevitable. History isn't made by great men or important battles. Human desire and activity is quite futile in itself, compared to the power of the stream of history.

However, notwithstanding the claimed inevitability of the movement of history and of its ultimate outcome, communism also offers a plan of attack: a political program for the working class organized by the communist political movement. This program will help it in its struggle for the world of freedom. Necessary evolution is linked to political revolution. This political revolution will be, like the politics of the current ruling class (the bourgeoisie, the capitalist employers of the working class), a product of some historically very specific economic circumstances. It will not and cannot take place without these circumstances. But it is also the result of a political program called "communism", of communist political organization, mobilization, leadership, propaganda, etc. These are some of the strange tensions within communist theory that we will explore later on.

Ideology

But let's slow down a bit and return for a moment to the communist analysis of the current world, which is still pre-communist according to the theory. Capitalism is still very much alive today. It covers practically the whole world since it has replaced the communist experiments in the 1990s, in the ex-USSR, in China, and in the countries previously allied to or occupied by these two major powers. The current economic crisis hasn't convinced many to give up the main elements of capitalism (private property, free markets, free trade, competition, rule of law, etc.) or to doubt the long-term viability of the system.

The concept of "ideology" plays an important part in the communist analysis of the world. An ideology pretends to be a description of the world but in reality it masks certain key aspects of it in order to maintain the economic status quo. It is an instrument in the continuation of the existing social order. It helps those who may threaten the status quo to forget the elements of their existence which can produce feelings of revolt.

Those who benefit from the existing order and who are therefore part of the ruling class, will tend to produce and propagate ideologies. "It is in this sense of ideas propagated to serve a particular class interest that Marx usually uses the term 'ideology'."[1] An ideology is part of the superstructure, just like politics, and is, like the whole superstructure, determined by the economic substructure and by class interest.

Religion

Religion is an example of an ideology. Desires that can harm the existing order and the status quo must be neutral-

---

1 D. McLellan, *The Thought of Karl Marx, Second Edition*, MacMillan, London, Basingstoke, 1986, p. 135.

ized. The idea of the Christian paradise expresses certain desires for a better world but makes it impossible to realize them and to threaten the existing order. By convincing people that these desires can only be realized in the afterlife, the idea or better ideology of paradise pacifies relationships in this life. Why revolt if you know that happiness is there for the taking in a future life? Especially when you will only get it if you respect morality in this life and when morality is often and conveniently incompatible with the consequences of revolt.

This ideology neutralizes desires by situating them in the afterlife. Religion is opium for the people, in the literal sense of the word. It's a drug that makes them forget the pain of this world, or at least convinces them to tolerate this pain, because pain can lead to revolt and those in power never like revolt. Christianity, according to Marx, is communism without the necessary revolutionary component. "Marx viewed ... religion as a statement of man's ideal aims and also a compensation for their lack of realization".[1]

Ideologies always want to produce acceptance of the status quo. They often express the desire for change but in such a way that this desire is neutralized and innocuous. Christianity shows a world of freedom, but does not allow its realization because it situates this freedom in another world. The purpose is that the Christian reconciles himself to a life of slavery and oppression. Because of his believe in salvation by God, he will not look for manmade salvation. Given the aforementioned stabilizing role of politics, it is not surprising that politics uses ideologies a lot.

Marx demanded that the ideals and protests that are implicit in ideologies such as Christianity are preserved but also transformed into revolutionary action. Ideologies should

1 Ibid., p. 207.

be exposed as ideologies, as illusions. The loss of illusions will create revolt that will destroy a situation that requires illusions.

> "The abolition of religion as the illusory happiness of men, is a demand for their real happiness. The call to abandon their illusions about their condition is a call to abandon a condition that requires illusions. The criticism of religion is, therefore, the embryonic criticism of this vale of tears of which religion is the halo. Criticism [of religion] has plucked the imaginary flowers from the chain, not in order that man shall bear the chain without caprice or consolation but so that he shall cast off the chain and pluck the living flower. The criticism of religion disillusions man so that he will think, act and fashion his reality as a man who has lost his illusions and regained his reason".[1]

Revolt will create a new and higher reality. Part of communist political action should therefore be criticism of religion and other ideologies. "The criticism of religion ends with the doctrine that man is the Supreme Being for man. It ends, therefore, with the categorical imperative to overthrow all those conditions in which man is an abased, enslaved, abandoned, contemptible being".[2] Ideologies will then no longer be necessary in this new world, because "they serve to reconcile the slave to the reality of his lack of freedom".[3]

Different Kinds of Rule

The existence of ideologies shows that class rule is not only a power thing. People are not only held down by force. Their minds are fashioned in such a way that they believe the ruling ideologies, and this incites them to accept the existing order, or at least to avoid revolt. An ideology is false

1 K. Marx, *Contribution to the Critique of Hegel's Philosophy of Right*, in R.C. Tucker, *The Marx-Engels Reader*, W.W. Norton, New York/London, 1978, p. 54.

2 Ibid., p. 60.

3 F. Fukuyama, *The End of History and the Last Man*, Penguin Books, Harmondsworth, 1992, p. 195.

consciousness: people think that they think, but in fact they think the thoughts of others, others in whose interest it is that they think these thoughts.

Class rule is an economic rule, an ideological rule, but also a political rule. Ideology is not always sufficient to maintain economic rule. Political force is often necessary. Politics and the state, the judges, the law and the police also serve the continuation of the existing economic rule. The ruling economic class uses the instruments of the state to serve its interests and to oppress the other classes, even if this state is a democracy.

Political rule is class rule by definition, in every political system. "The state power is nothing more than the organization with which the ruling classes — landlords and capitalists — have provided themselves in order to protect their social privileges".[1] "The executive of the modern State is but a committee for managing the common affairs of the whole

---

1 F. Engels, *Letter to Th. Cuno*, in R.C. Tucker, op. cit., p. 728. See also the following citations: "the State is the form in which the individuals of a ruling class assert their common interests", K. Marx, *The German Ideology*, in R.C. Tucker, op. cit., p. 187; "capitalist society and ... the state institutions which it had brought into being", F. Engels, *Speech at the Graveside of Karl Marx*, in R.C. Tucker, op. cit., p. 682; "Der moderne Staat ist ... die Organisation, die sich die bürgerliche Gesellschaft gibt, um die allgemeinen äusseren Bedingungen der kapitalistischen Produktionsweise aufrecht zu erhalten gegen Uebergriffe sowohl der Arbeiter, wie der einzelnen Kapitalisten. Der moderne Staat, was auch seine Form, ist also eine wesentlich kapitalistische Maschine, Staat der Kapitalisten, der ideelle Gesammtkapitalist ... d.h. eine Organisation der jedesmaligen ausbeutenden Klasse zur Aufrechterhaltung ihrer äussern Produktionsbedingungen, also namentlich zur gewaltsamen Niederhaltung der ausgebeuteten Klasse in den durch die bestehende Produktionsweise gegebenen Bedingungen der Unterdrückung", F. Engels, *Anti-Dühring*, in *Marx-Engels Gesamtausgabe, I, 27*, Dietz Verlag, Berlin, 1988, p. 443-444; "the State ... is nothing more than the form of organization which the bourgeois necessarily adopt both for internal and external purposes, for the mutual guarantee of their property and interests... . the State exists only for the sake of private property", K. Marx, *The German Ideology*, in R.C. Tucker, op. cit., p. 187.

---

bourgeoisie".[1] Politics is therefore no more than violence that is used to oppress. Violence and the possession of the means of violence is for communism the single most important characteristic of government and the political domain.[2]

Substructure and Superstructure

Those were a few words about the so-called superstructure that sits on top of and is determined by the substructure. The substructure, according to communism, is the mode of production or the nature of productive activity. Productive activity means the production, in interaction with nature, of goods necessary to survive. This production requires, on the one hand, means of production (materials, machines, land, tools, labor, etc.) and, on the other hand, relations in which production takes place (relations of co-operation or ways of organization such as relations between masters and slaves, employers and employees, landowners and farmers, etc.). The combination of means (or forces) of production and relations of production is the mode of production.

The available means of production determine the relations of production. A certain degree of development in the former necessarily produces a certain degree of development in the latter. This idea is the basis of the historical evolution of society that is so important in communism.

> "In production, men not only act on nature but also on one another. They produce only by co-operating in a certain way and mutually exchanging their activities. In order to produce, they enter into definite connections and relations with one another and only within these social connections and relations does their action on nature, does production, take place. These social relations into which the producers enter with one another, the conditions under which they exchange their ac-

1 Marx, Engels, *The Communist Manifesto*, Penguin Books, Harmondsworth, 1985, p. 82.

2 H. Arendt, *La crise de la culture*, Gallimard, Paris, 1992, p. 34-35.

tivities and participate in the whole act of production, will naturally vary according to the character of the means of production. With the invention of a new instrument of warfare, firearms, the whole internal organization of the army necessarily changed: the relationships within which individuals can constitute an army and act as an army were transformed ... Thus the social relations within which individuals produce, the social relations of production, change, are transformed, with the change and development of the material means of production, the productive forces".[1]

These social relations are therefore independent of the will of the participants. They depend on technology, the availability of land, etc. Each major change in the relations of production and the organization of production, caused by changes in the means of production, leads to a major change in the type of society we live in.

The combination of means of production or productive forces on the one hand, and relations of production on the other, is the substructure and determines the superstructure or the collection of different forms of consciousness, such as law, morality, religion, philosophy, politics, etc.

The substructure is "the real foundation, on which rises a legal and political superstructure and to which correspond definite forms of social consciousness".[2] "Economic production and the structure of society of every historical epoch necessarily arising therefrom constitute the foundation for the political and intellectual history of that epoch".[3]

1 K. Marx, *Wage Labor and Capital (1849)*, in D. McLellan, *The Thought of Karl Marx*, op. cit., p. 142-143.

2 K. Marx, *Preface to A Contribution to the Critique of Political Economy*, in R.C. Tucker, op. cit., p. 4.

3 Marx, Engels, *The Communist Manifesto*, op. cit., p. 57.

Figure 1: Substructure or Mode of Production

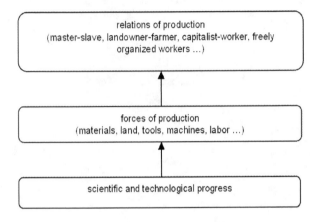

Substructure and Human Rights

As mentioned before, politics and law are parts of the superstructure which are determined by the substructure. They are formed by the interests of those who have economic power and they serve to defend these interests. "Political power ... is merely the organized power of one class for oppressing another".[1] "Are economic relations regulated by legal conceptions or do not, on the contrary, legal relations arise from economic ones?"[2] The quintessential example is the right to private property. Owners can use this right to defend their interests against the poor. They can appeal to the judiciary and the police force to defend their property and hence to maintain existing class relations and modes of production.

The right to private property makes it impossible for large groups of people to have their own means of production and

---

1 Ibid., p. 105.
2 K. Marx, *Critique of the Gotha Program*, in R.C. Tucker, op. cit., p. 528.

hence to be economically independent and self-sufficient. In other words, it makes it impossible for people to be free.

However, the law is not only something that can be used to justify the use of force for the maintenance of the status quo. The use of force by the state for the defense of the right to property is not necessary when the poor can be convinced that this right is in their interest, that it is a *human* right rather than a right of the wealthy. The economic relationships and structures are maintained with political and legal force but also with legal ideology.

All ideologies are similar. Christianity can convince people to accept their situation by promising salvation in a future life, and the ideology of human rights does the same by convincing people, all people, that they have the same rights and that they are therefore equal. When this universality and equality of rights is accentuated, people do not see that others who have the same equal rights profit more from these rights. Human rights give the impression of guaranteeing freedom and equality but in reality give those who are better off tools to improve their situation even more, and at the expense of the poor. Instead of real equality there is only legal and formal equality, and the latter takes us further away from the former because the rich can use their equal rights to promote their interests. Rights give us the freedom to oppress rather than freedom from oppression.

Human rights, according to communism, are "an illusory sense of community serving as a screen for the real struggles waged by classes against each other",[1] an ideological veil on reality, a set of false ideas that has to cover up class rule and make it acceptable. The continuation of inequality by political and legal means is based on the combination of coercion and false consciousness. Christians are equal in heaven and

---

[1] D. McLellan, *Marx*, Fontana Press, London, 1986, p. 60.

thereby maintain inequality on earth, and believers in human rights are equal in the heaven of their political ideals and thereby forget the inequality that these ideals help to maintain. Again we see how the ruling class uses ideology rather than mere force to maintain its rule. It tries to instill certain beliefs in its victims and to use these beliefs as a drug, an opium to pacify them.

Like the protest inherent in the Christian ideology of a future paradise must be maintained but stripped of its ideological content, so the ideal of equality inherent in human rights must be maintained but in such a way that it becomes real equality in a real and worldly paradise, and not some kind of formal equality of rights that only aggravates real inequality and postpones paradise to the afterlife. The poor must become conscious of the fact that their formal equality only covers up their real inequality. This consciousness will be an important step in their liberation. However, as we will see later, this consciousness is conditioned by and can only come about at a certain time in the evolution of exploitation. It cannot result from education or political agitation alone.

Substructure and the Mind

The creation and propagation of ideology is therefore an important activity of the ruling class. The members of this class usually do not work but appropriate the fruits of the labor of other classes, and hence they have the necessary leisure time to engage in intellectual "work" and to construct and promote ideologies that they can use to serve their interests, consciously or unconsciously. Those with material power also have intellectual power. They can influence what others think, and they will be most successful if they themselves believe the ideologies that they want to force on others.

This clearly shows that the substructure does not only determine the legal and political parts of the superstructure, but thinking as well. The prevailing ideas are the ideas of the prevailing class.

> "[T]he class which is the ruling material force of society, is at the same time its ruling intellectual force. The class which has the means of material production at its disposal, has control at the same time over the means of mental production, so that thereby, generally speaking, the ideas of those who lack the means of mental production are subject to it. The ruling ideas are nothing more than the ideal expression of the dominant material relationships, the dominant material relationships grasped as ideas; hence of the relationships which make the one class the ruling one, therefore, the ideas of its dominance. The individuals composing the ruling class possess among other things consciousness, and therefore think. Insofar, therefore, as they rule as a class and determine the extent and compass of an epoch, it is self-evident that they do this in its whole range, hence among other things rule also as thinkers, as producers of ideas, and regulate the production and distribution of the ideas of their age: thus their ideas are the ruling ideas of the epoch".[1]

But there is a kind of feedback action at work here. The substructure determines ideas, but these ideas in turn help to maintain a particular economic substructure. Not everything goes up from the material to the intellectual. Something comes down as well, but only after it went up first.

This can be expressed in the left half of the following drawing:

---

1 K. Marx, *The German Ideology*, in R.C. Tucker, op. cit., p. 172-173.

Figure 2: Sources of Determination

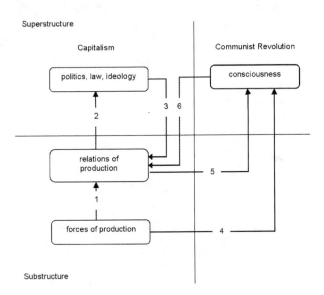

In this drawing, an arrow means "determination". All ideas, not only political and legal ones, are both the expression (arrow 2) and the safeguard (arrow 3) of the economic structure of society. (The bottom-left half, arrow 1, represents the previously mentioned relationship between means of production and relations of production, see also figure 1).

But there is also a right half in this drawing: the fact that ideas, in a kind of feedback mode, help to determine a particular economic structure, does not always have to be negative or aimed at the status quo. The poor, when they shed their false consciousness imposed by ideology, become conscious of their real situation, and this consciousness will help to start the revolution which will modify class relations and hence the substructure. This is represented by arrow 6.

Ideally, arrow 6 would have to pass through the box containing "politics" since the revolutionary proletariat will take over the state when attempting to modify the relations of production.

However, as we will see below, this awakening is bound to certain material preconditions, in particular the presence of certain very specific forces of production, namely large-scale industrial production with mass labor (arrow 4) and the strain imposed by existing class relations (arrow 5). It cannot, therefore, take place in every setting. Ultimately, all consciousness, real and false, is determined by the substructure. The order of determinations is fixed and follows the numerical order in the drawing.

Evolving Politics

In line with the communist insistence on determination, politics, as a reflection of the substructure, must evolve with the substructure. This is true for both capitalist and communist politics.

> "The fact is ... that definite individuals who are productively active in a definite way enter into these definite social and political relations. Empirical observation must in each separate instance bring out empirically, and without any mystification and speculation, the connection of the social and political structure with production. The social structure and the State are continually evolving out of the life process of definite individuals, but of individuals, not as they may appear in their own or other people's imagination, but as they really are; i.e., as they operate, produce materially, and hence as they work under definite material limits, presuppositions and conditions independent of their will".[1]

> "[L]egal relations as well as forms of state are to be grasped neither from themselves nor from the so-called

---

1 K. Marx, *The German Ideology*, in R.C. Tucker, op. cit., p. 154.

general development of the human mind, but rather have their roots in the material conditions of life".[1]

As these conditions evolve, politics and the law must evolve as well. Politics and all that it entails (war, revolutions, diplomacy, etc.) are not the motor of history. The evolution of the modes of production determines the evolution of everything else. Every new mode of production causes a change in politics, often with some delay.

The feudal mode of production entailed the political rule of the nobility and the landowners. Those who ruled production and owned the means of production (land, cattle, etc.) also ruled politically. Industrialization, driven by technology and science, caused a modification of the mode of production and the relations of production, and, with some delay, caused the replacement of those in power. The bourgeoisie, the owners of industry, took over from the nobility because they had the financial resources and the commercial spirit to appropriate the new industrial means of production. And a new leader in production became a new political leader, in France by way of a political revolution, in England by way of the incorporation of the nobility into the bourgeoisie.

During the first stages of industrialization in France, the political power continued to belong to the nobility, but the evolving economic conditions turned the unchanged political situation into an anachronism. A feudal political structure continued to encapsulate an economic system that had abandoned feudal production long ago. Politics had turned into a constraint on production (e.g., local bastions of nobility with their own particular rules and taxes inhibiting commerce as an integral part of industrial production). The French Revolution, an explosion resulting from a build-up of tension between politics and the economy, discarded this old political

---

[1] K. Marx, *Preface to A Contribution to the Critique of Political Economy*, in R.C. Tucker, op. cit., p. 4.

garbage and created a new, national and republican political order.

One day, communists hope or rather know, production will evolve in such a way that the bourgeoisie will find itself in the same situation as the nobility in 18th century France. Nothing that happens in this manner is voluntary. The forces of production outgrow those who profit from them and who own political power because of them. These forces of production drive whole societies from one stage of development to another, without the active prodding of anyone, and without anyone being able to stop it.

Power and Ownership of the Means of Production

According to communism, the ownership of the means of production determines economic rule and economic rule determines political rule. If you own the means of production, then other people depend on you for their subsistence. They cannot produce goods themselves because they don't have means of production, and hence have to sell their labor power to you in order to survive. You may decide not to buy their labor or to buy the labor of someone else. You can use workers' dependence and competition to depress the price of labor, which creates poverty for the working class and wealth for your own class. This is economic rule based on ownership.

Compared to an old-fashioned subsistence economy, fewer and fewer people own means of production in an industrial capitalist economy. The means of production have become so large and expensive that practically no-one can own them. Economic dependence becomes the rule in this system.

> "[T]he man who possesses no other property than his labor power must, in all conditions of society and culture, be the slave of other men who have made themselves the owners of the material conditions of labor. He can work only with their permission, hence live only with their permission".[1]

However, this economic rule of a few capitalists, able to own the means of production, over the large majority of dependent workers, may be fragile because workers can join forces against the capitalists. Hence the latter may also need political and intellectual power to reinforce and guarantee their economic power. They use laws, the police, the justice system and ideology to keep workers in submission. They can quite easily acquire political power because they have the financial means and the ideological means to do so. They can acquire ideological power because they have finances, leisure and education. Also in a democracy, in which supposedly the people rule, do we see that the minority of owners of the means of production use their financial means to corrupt the process to their advantage.

Given the trend in industrial technology, communism expects that the scale of production will become ever larger. This will result in an ever smaller number of owners of the means of production. Dependence will become unbearable and the system will explode. Large-scale production will also sow the seeds of labor organization and unionization, and will fasten the downfall of capitalism. I'll come back to this.

The Mind and the Futility of Individuality

In communism, the mind is the product of matter. Thinking reflects and is determined, conditioned, even produced by the substructure of economic reality. And this is true for both the so-called false consciousness under capitalism and the

---

1 K. Marx, *Critique of the Gotha Program*, in R.C. Tucker, op. cit., p. 526.

awakening of the communist workers. "The mode of production of material life conditions the social, political and intellectual life process in general".[1]

> "Your very ideas [bourgeois ideas] are but the outgrowth of the conditions of your bourgeois production and bourgeois property, just as your jurisprudence is but the will of your class made into a law for all, a will, whose essential character and direction are determined by the economical conditions of existence of your class. The selfish misconception that induces you to transform into eternal laws of nature and of reason, the social forms springing from your present mode of production and form of property — historical relations that rise and disappear in the progress of production — this misconception you share with every ruling class that has preceded you".[2] "Does it require deep intuition to comprehend that man's ideas, views and conceptions, in one word, man's consciousness, changes with every change in the conditions of his material existence, in his social relations and in his social life? What else does the history of ideas prove, than that intellectual production changes in character in proportion as material production is changed?"[3]

Thinking is not an independent activity, let alone the motor of history. Material changes create mental changes and not vice versa. Communism does not explain practice from ideas but explains the formation of ideas from material practice. "It is not the consciousness of men that determines their being, but, on the contrary, their social being that determines their consciousness".[4]

The same is true for the thinking of the working class. We'll see later on that it is the evolution of the means of production and the practice of increasing oppression and exploitation which will force the workers to abandon their false

1 K. Marx, *Preface to A Contribution to the Critique of Political Economy*, in R.C. Tucker, op. cit., p. 4.

2 Marx, Engels, *The Communist Manifesto*, op. cit., p. 99-100.

3 Ibid., p. 102.

4 K. Marx, *Preface to A Contribution to the Critique of Political Economy*, in R.C. Tucker, op. cit., p. 4.

consciousness and to gain insight in their situation and in the only possible future. This insight will react back on material reality by revolutionizing it, but only after it has been determined first by material reality.

Hence there is only an apparent contradiction between, on the one hand, the statement that material changes create mental changes (and not vice versa) and, on the other hand, the need for revolution inspired by communist theory. The material world is the motor of history, but ideas which are produced by the material world can feedback into the material world and produce change. However, the real and original cause of change remains the material world, because only a certain stage of development of this world allows for the apparition of certain ideas.

Figure 3: Ideas at a Certain Stage of Material Development

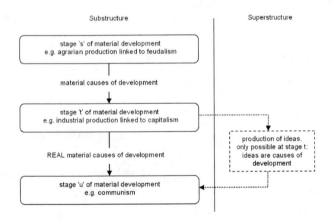

Communism, like bourgeois ideology and every other theory, is a product of the economy, but a product only of an economy that has reached a certain level of development.

Marx was adamant that communist society cannot come before its time. Attempting a communist revolution when the mode of production hasn't evolved to a certain point, is futile.

Here are some examples of the way in which matter determines the mind according to communism.

> "It is a well-known fact that Greek mythology was not only the arsenal of Greek art, but also the very ground from which it had sprung. Is the view of nature and of social relations which shaped Greek imagination and Greek art possible in the age of automatic machinery and railways and locomotives and electric telegraphs? ... All mythology masters and dominates and shapes the forces of nature in and through the imagination; hence it disappears as soon as man gains mastery over the forces of nature ... Greek art presupposes the existence of Greek mythology, i.e., that nature and even the form of society are wrought up in popular fancy in an unconsciously artistic fashion. That is its material. Not, however, any mythology taken at random, nor any accidental unconsciously artistic elaboration of nature (including under the latter all objects, hence also society). Egyptian mythology could never be the soil or womb which would give birth to Greek art. But in any event there had to be a mythology. In no event could Greek art originate in a society which excludes any mythological explanation of nature, any mythological attitude towards it, or which requires of the artist an imagination free from mythology. Looking at it from another side: is Achilles possible side by side with powder and lead? Or is the Iliad at all compatible with the printing press and even printing machines? Do not singing and reciting and the muses necessarily go out of existence with the appearance of the printer's bar, and do not, therefore, the prerequisites of epic poetry disappear?"[1]

Greek mythology, which was the basis of Greek art, was only possible within the ancient mode of production. Therefore Greek art was only possible in that mode of production and impossible in any mode of production that implied

---

[1] K. Marx, *Grundrisse*, in D. McLellan, *The Thought of Karl Marx*, op. cit., p. 144-145.

a better control of nature (such as the industrial mode of production).

Now regarding another part of the mind, namely morality:

"[W]hen we see that the three classes of modern society, the feudal aristocracy, the bourgeoisie and the proletariat, each have a morality of their own, we can only draw the one conclusion: that men, consciously or unconsciously, derive their ethical ideas in the last resort from the practical relations on which their class position is based — from the economic relations in which they carry on production and exchange ... We maintain ... that all moral theories have been hitherto the product, in the last analysis, of the economic conditions of society obtaining at the time".[1]

"The production of ideas, of conceptions, of consciousness, is at first directly interwoven with the material activity and the material intercourse of men, the language of real life. Conceiving, thinking, the mental intercourse of men, appear at this stage as the direct efflux of their material behavior. The same applies to mental production as expressed in the language of politics, laws, morality, religion, metaphysics, etc., of a people. Men are the producers of their conceptions, ideas, etc. — real, active men, as they are conditioned by a definite development of their productive forces and of the intercourse corresponding to these, up to its furthest forms ... we do not set out from what men say, imagine, conceive, nor from men as narrated, thought of, imagined, conceived, in order to arrive at men in the flesh. We set out from real, active men, and on the basis of their real life-process we demonstrate the development of the ideological reflexes and echoes of this life-process. The phantoms formed in the human brain are also, necessarily, sublimates of their material life-process, which is empirically verifiable and bound to material premises. Morality, religion, metaphysics, all the rest of ideology and their corresponding forms of consciousness, thus no longer retain the semblance of independence. They have no history, no development; but men, developing their material production and their material intercourse, alter, along with this their real existence, their thinking and the products of their

---

1 F. Engels, *Anti-Dühring*, in R.C. Tucker, op. cit., p. 726.

thinking. Life is not determined by consciousness, but consciousness by life".[1]

When thinking is determined by production, then individual identity is as well because an individual identity is a collection of thoughts and feelings.

> "[The] mode of production must not be considered simply as being the reproduction of the physical existence of the individuals. Rather it is a definite form of activity of these individuals, a definite form of expressing their life, a definite mode of life on their part. As individuals express their life, so they are. What they are, therefore, coincides with their production, both with what they produce and with how they produce. The nature of individuals thus depends on the material conditions determining their production".[2]

Personality is not something which is created in freedom and autonomy. It is determined by outside forces, material forces. "We do not mean it to be understood ... that, for example, the rentier, the capitalist, etc., cease to be persons; but their personality is conditioned and determined by quite definite class relationships".[3]

The individual is just a specimen of something larger. He or she is a representative of a class, representative not simply in the sense of representing the interests of a class, but also in the sense of being equal to and having the same basic personality as all other members of the class. "Individuals are dealt with only in so far as they are the personifications of economic categories, bearers of particular class-relations and class-interests".[4] Not the individual with his or her personal characteristics is important, but the collective class identity.

---

1 K. Marx, *The German Ideology*, in R.C. Tucker, op. cit., p. 154-155.

2 Ibid., p. 150.

3 Ibid., p. 199.

4 K. Marx, *Capital, A Student Edition*, Lawrence & Wishart, London, 1992, p. xxiv.

Chapter 2. To The Realm of Freedom

Dogmatic Optimism and Utopian Fatalism

The goal of communism, communist society, also called the Realm of Freedom, is the next and inevitable step in the evolution of society after capitalism. Capitalism is doomed and will be replaced by communism. We'll see later why this is certain in the eyes of communists and why there is no alternative. In a few words, it will come down to this: their situation will become so desperate that the workers must gain consciousness and start the communist revolution which will inaugurate a new and final step in the evolution of society. With the progress of science and industry, the forces of production will develop in such a way that worker organization and solidarity are encouraged and that communist production is the only viable option.

The end of history will be reached, utopia will be realized. Communist theory is a kind of utopian fatalism. Utopia must and will come, whatever happens. It is an inescapable ideal and a communist is a dogmatic optimist. The goal which he or she aspires to, will be reached. It is not even an aspiration, a wish, or a desire, or at least not necessarily. Even if nobody aspires to it, it will happen, of itself, automatically and necessarily.

Communist Science

Notwithstanding the importance of the ideal, communist theory focuses more on the steps towards it than on the description of utopia, which is after all the realm of freedom and hence indescribable by definition. It sees a stepwise evolution in history, one phase of development following and transcending another, often with revolutions in-between. This development has a force similar to the force exercised by the laws of nature. It is inevitable, unstoppable and irreversible. History follows a necessary path. Independently of the wills and actions of people, history goes towards a certain destination. Hence the talk about "laws of history" or the "laws of historical development". The theory which describes this evolution and these laws, communism, does nothing but this: describe. Communist society is not a desire but a prediction based on the scientific description of history, of the laws of history and of the current situation.

This focus on prediction based on description is the reason behind the claim that communism is a science. Only a science can make predictions. Communism believes that a scientific analysis of historical development can unearth laws of development which in turn can serve to predict future development, much like the study of the path of comets in the present and the past can be used to predict their future path. The ultimate goal of a development can be gauged by looking at its past, "interpreting the past, in order to predict the future".[1]

The dispassionate belief in evolution, the irrelevance of desires, and the claim of science are all typical of communism and could not be found in previous utopian theories.

> "The novelty which Marx provided, according to his own account, was to show how the ideal future would grow out of the practical present. There was no need to postulate some impossible change of heart. Dialectical materialism would compel men to live in Utopia whatever the promptings of their hearts".[2]

Utopia is not in the first instance the product of human reason, brotherly love or good will, or of conscious strategy and action. It is the consequence of the laws of historical development. It is the necessary conclusion of what is already happening.

At first sight, this limits our role to that of spectators. If our desires go against the course of history and the laws of its development, then they are futile. If they do not, they are futile as well, because history goes its way even without them. The goal of history is completely independent of our wishes. The latter are reasonable only if they are in harmony with history. But even if they are reasonable, they are not necessarily influential.

However, this is not what communism claims. Wishes are important, but only to the extent that they are based on and the product of changes in economic reality (see figures 2 and 3 above). They can slow down or fasten historical evolution. If our wishes correspond to historical development, they may fasten it, but the development will take place even without them. A certain stage of historical development produces certain ideas, ideas which can only be produced at and by this stage. These economically determined ideas will then be one

1 K. Popper, *The Poverty of Historicism*, Routledge, London, 1995, p. 50.
2 A. J. P. Taylor, *Introduction to the Communist Manifesto*, op. cit., p. 9-10.

of the many "economic" forces behind the passing to the next stage.

History and Post-History

Some of the Jewish and Christian tradition is reflected in the communist certainty of the destination of history. The vale of tears has become the oppression of the workers caused by the division of society in classes of owners and non-owners, in turn caused by private property. This vale of tears is now called the realm of necessity. Paradise has become communism or the realm of freedom.

There is even something which corresponds to the Fall of Man: Marx and Engels sometimes talk about the introduction of private property as if it was the original sin, fracturing original societies characterized by some kind of original communism (community of property) and introducing the rule of man over man. However, communism is never nostalgic. This beginning of history was not a real Paradise because people still lived under the yoke of nature. They did not have the blessings of technology and industry. The goal is not a return to the past. True freedom is a thing of the future.

All history since this Fall of Man has been characterized by the combined oppression by man and nature, by class struggle between slaves and masters, be they literally slaves and masters, or landless farmers and feudal lords, or proletarian workers and capitalists.

In both communism and western religion, history has a definite purpose and even an ending, and history and society as a whole move towards that end. In fact; there is a history and a post-history, a lower and a higher kind of life. Rather ironic given the communist aversion of religion. The difference is that communism turns the transcendent into the immanent. Salvation has become a worldly goal.

Exploitation and Surplus Value

In capitalism, a certain stage of evolution in the vale of tears, oppression means, among other things, expropriation of surplus value. The capitalists or the bourgeoisie are the ruling class and the owners of the forces of production (machines, soil, buildings, infrastructure, etc.) and therefore are "the monopolizer[s] of the means of labor, that is, the sources of life".[1]

This monopoly does not only create dependence for the workers; it also means exploitation. The workers are the majority of the people. "[S]tanding over against [the] productive forces, we have the majority of the individuals from whom these forces have been wrested away".[2] They are exploited because the surplus value — a worker creates more value in a day than he gets paid — is taken by the capitalist. Or, in other words: "The wages of the laborer had a smaller exchange-value than the exchange value of the object he produced".[3] The object is sold by the capitalist, who buys labor and pockets the difference. "[T]he workers would produce values that exceeded the reimbursement of their labor".[4]

The capitalist forces the worker to work more than the hours necessary to embody in his product the value of his labor power. For example, if the value of labor power, i.e., the wage, is $50 a day, and a worker produces a good (or goods) which is worth $100 during a full day of work, then the sec-

---

1 K. Marx, *Critique of the Gotha Program*, in R.C. Tucker, op. cit., p. 527.
2 K. Marx, *The German Ideology*, in R.C. Tucker, op. cit., p. 190.
3 D. McLellan, *Marx*, op. cit., p. 52.
4 Ibid., p. 55.

ond half of the day would yield surplus value, in this case an-other $50.

This is theft, because the capitalist takes something which he has not produced. He takes the unpaid labor and products of someone else and lives on the back of someone else, simply because he has the privilege of owning the means of production. The workers have to accept this because they depend on the capitalist. They have to sell their labor power in order to survive because they do not own means of produc-tion and hence cannot produce and live without the consent of the capitalists. As the workers' energy is not depleted after their own reproduction is guaranteed — through the pay-ment of a wage — one can use it to produce more.

Moreover, the capitalist continuously tries to maximize his surplus value. He uses technology and science to increase productivity and diminish the necessary labor time per unit of production. Machines allow him to produce more with less labor. If wages stay constant and productivity goes up, then surplus value goes up.

But wages, of course, do not stay constant. The capitalist also tries to make labor as cheap as possible and the working day as long as possible.[1] This is another kind of oppression, different from but inextricably linked to the expropriation of surplus value. This is achieved by way of the so-called "indus-trial reserve army". This is a relatively large group, constantly available but not necessarily made up of the same people> They are unemployed, desperate to work, ready to replace the employed and ready to accept a lower wage and a longer working day. This reserve army is a millstone round the neck of the proletariat, a regulator keeping wages at a low level.[2]

---

[1] By the way, there are also other ways to maximize surplus-value: im-ports of cheap commodities by way of colonial exploitation; a better and more efficient organization of production (co-operation, divi-sion of labor ...).

[2] F. Engels, *Anti-Dühring*, op. cit., p. 440.

"[T]he wage-worker has permission to work for his own subsistence, that is, to live, only in so far as he works for a certain time gratis for the capitalist (and hence also for the latter's co-consumers of surplus value); ... the whole capitalist system of production turns on the increase of this gratis labor by extending the working day or by developing the productivity, that is, increasing the intensity of labor power, etc." [1]

The capitalist accumulates surplus value and wealth, and the worker accumulates misery. "[P]overty and destitution develop among the workers, and wealth and culture among the non-workers. This is the law of all history hitherto". [2] The "immiserization" ("Verelendung") of the proletariat is something relative:

"Marx was usually wary of claiming that the proletariat would become immiserized in any absolute sense. Such an idea would not have harmonized well with his view of all human needs as mediated through society. What he did claim was that the gap in resources between those who owned the means of production and those who did not would widen". [3]

"Everywhere the great mass of the working classes were sinking down to a lower depth, at the same rate at least, that those above them were rising in the social scale. In all countries of Europe it has now become a truth demonstrable to every unprejudiced mind, and only denied by those, whose interest it is to hedge other people in a fool's paradise, that no improvement of machinery, no appliance of science to production, no contrivances of communication, no new colonies, no emigration, no opening of markets, no free trade, nor all these things put together, will do away with the miseries of the industrious masses; but that, on the present false base, every fresh development of the productive powers of labor must tend to deepen social contrasts and point social antagonisms". [4]

---

1 K. Marx, *Critique of the Gotha Program*, in R.C. Tucker, op. cit., p. 535.

2 Ibid., p. 527.

3 D. McLellan, *Marx*, op. cit., p. 44.

4 K. Marx, *Inaugural Address of the Working Men's International Association*, in R.C. Tucker, op. cit., p. 516.

Figure 4: Maximization of Surplus-Value

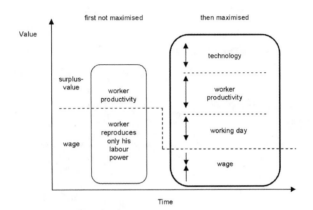

We will see later how the maximization of surplus value deepens social divisions, brings despair to the workers, and hence will contribute to the collapse of capitalism. Wages will fall below the subsistence level (as is depicted in figure 4) and the working day and the requirements of productivity will go beyond what is humanly bearable.

The Price for the Regeneration of Labor Power

According to communism, the value of something (or its price or exchange rate) is determined by the labor force and the labor time that went into it, that were necessary to produce it.[1] Value does not depend on the use one makes of some-

---

1 From an economic point of view, this is the main weakness of communist theory. "[T]he proposition that commodities will tend to exchange at their labour values is false", *Marxian Economics*, W.W. Norton, New York/London, 1990. However, I will not return to this

thing, on the price the market is willing to pay, etc. If I buy a chair and I tell the carpenter that I want to use the chair as wood for my fireplace and hence can only pay one tenth of the price, then this person will tell me that I need to pay his labor. At least his labor, preferably with a profit.

It is therefore only the amount of work or labor time necessary for the production of something that determines its value.[1] Every value, even the value of labor or labor power itself, is determined in this way. This labor power is sold by the worker to the capitalist. The value of labor power, or the wage paid by the capitalist to the worker, is determined by the value of the goods necessary to produce this labor power, or, in other words, by the value of the goods necessary to enable the worker to work.

If a worker needs $50 a day to survive in such a way that he can regenerate his labor power, then $50 is the price of labor and hence the wage. All the value that the worker produces on top of that $50 during that day is surplus value for the capitalist. The worker produces his labor power by reproducing himself and conserving his life in a manner that allows him to work.

> "For his maintenance he requires a given quantity of the means of subsistence. Therefore the labor-time requisite for the production of labor-power reduces itself to that necessary for the production of those means of subsistence; in other words, the value of labor-power is the value of the means of subsistence necessary for the maintenance of the laborer".[2]

The worker can only work if he consumes certain goods, goods that have a value. The amount of labor incorporated into these goods determines the value of the labor power of

---

problem in the evaluation chapter, because, for my purposes, it's one of secondary importance.

1 K. Marx, in F. Chatelet, *Le Capital, Profil d'une oeuvre*, Hatier, Paris, 1975, p. 42.

2 K. Marx, *Capital*, op. cit., p. 101.

the worker consuming them. According to communism, it is not the amount of labor that a worker produces per day which determines the value of his labor, because then there could be no surplus value.

The capitalist therefore buys the energy of the worker and pays him a reasonably correct price for it, initially, at least. If not, the worker would perish and his labor power would no longer be available. What he does not pay for correctly is the production of the worker. After four hours during a ten-hour working day, for example, the labor power of the average worker is already regenerated (because four hours of labor in this example are necessary to produce the goods that the average worker needs per day in order to regenerate his labor power). So the capitalist only pays for four hours. During the other six hours he gets free labor.

The worker's labor consists of two parts: one corresponds to the material reconstitution of the energy used, and the other is surplus work for which he is not paid. Hence, labor produces goods and surplus value, the origin of profit. This profit is based on labor which is stolen, not paid for.[1]

The capitalist does not pay for the production, the true value of the products of labor. He does not pay for all the work. He only pays for the part which the worker needs in order to be able to work again tomorrow. There is surplus value and hence profit because the price of one day of labor is less than the revenues generated by one day of labor. The price of one day of labor is the price of the goods necessary for the daily regeneration of labor power, and the price of these goods is less than the revenues produced by one day of labor.

The value of labor and the value that labor produces are two different things. During a part of the day, the worker produces nothing else than the value of his own labor power, i.e.,

---

1 F. Chatelet, op. cit., p. 49.

the value of the goods necessary for him to survive in such a way that he can work tomorrow, i.e., the value of his wage which he repays by working during that part of the day. Of course, he does not produce the goods he needs himself because he works in a system of division of labor. He produces, during a part of the day, a certain good which has a value that equals the value of his consumer goods.

However, because of economic competition or greed (or both), the capitalist will tend to push the price of labor below the value of it. The result is the further immiserization of the workers. I'll come back to that.

Intensification of the Class Struggle

The class struggle existed before capitalism because it is inherent in every society characterized by the unequal ownership of the means of production. Slave and feudal societies were class societies in which a surplus value was created by the workers and maximized and expropriated by the ruling classes. The owners of the means of production (mostly land and life-stock in those societies) already pushed the rest of the population into dependence because they could allow or disallow the use of these means of production. The condition of this use was always the creation and hand-over of surplus value.

In capitalism, however, we see that the production of surplus value is no longer a simple means for an easy life for the rich; it has become a goal in itself.[1] The creation of open markets (through new means of transport, trade liberalization, the creation of nation states, etc.) has led to fierce competition between capitalists. The creation and maximization of surplus value has become a matter of life and death for the

---

1 K. Marx, *Capital*, op. cit., p. 143-144.

capitalist. If he doesn't maximize, another one will and he will be out of business in no time.

The limitless maximization of surplus value in capitalism creates poverty, stress and oppression to such a degree that workers have no other option but revolution. (This is the meaning of arrow 5 in figure 2 above). "[P]overty should help men to break the shackles of oppression, because the poor have nothing to lose but their chains".[1] Oppression, poverty and class struggle will inevitably disappear because of their intensification. The nearer the dawn, the darker the light, or, in the words of Hölderlin: "Wo die Gefahr wächst, wächst das Rettende auch". "Danger and deliverance make their advances together".[2]

Capitalism is a phase of history about to end as a result of its internal contradictions and the fact that it has produced its own gravediggers, the proletariat. It destroys itself and ushers in a new and final phase of history. "This social formation [bourgeois society] brings, therefore, the prehistory of human society to a close"[3] and initiates true history. The new world of communism and freedom is not merely an ideal, a model which has to inspire people. It is the result of an evolution and a movement that are already happening. The seeds of it are already growing in today's rotten soil. Not "if" but "when" is the question. We will see later how man can speed up the process. Crucial for this will be the awakening of the proletariat. Their revolt, the necessary result of their situation, can be promoted, incited and organized.

Both communism and Christianity are examples of idealistic fatalism (or fatalistic idealism if you want). The advent of the ideal new world is certain. The difference is that,

---

1 H. Arendt, *On Revolution*, Penguin Books, Harmondsworth, 1990, p. 66.

2 Th. Paine, *The Crisis*, Penguin Books, Harmondsworth, 1995, p. 23.

3 K. Marx, *Preface to A Contribution to the Critique of Political Economy*, in R.C. Tucker, op. cit., p. 5.

in Christianity, access to the new world is a decision of God in the afterlife. Man can influence this decision by his individual actions (piety, prayer, caritas, repentance, etc.), but ultimately he cannot gain access independently. The advent of the new world isn't tied to historical conditions or a certain level of evolution of society. It is God's autonomous decision. In communism, the new world is the product of history and can be promoted by collective rather than individual action. Everyone, not only the devout, will have access. Even the ex-capitalists.

Labor, Nature, Freedom

The new world, the realm of freedom and the classless society, will put an end to the realm of necessity. It will liberate us, not only of oppression, dependence, exploitation and inequality, but also of necessity, necessity in the sense of the rule of natural needs. Labor as the activity which produces the goods that are necessary to fulfill our natural needs, or, in other words, the activity which reproduces life, will disappear. Labor will continue to exist, but it will no longer be a necessity imposed by nature. Instead it will be a free, creative, spontaneous and productive activity. Man will be free from the limits imposed by natural necessity, as he will be free from the dependence and exploitation inherent in wage labor. The capitalist as well will be freed from acquisitiveness and the drive to maximize profit.

In the realm of freedom, labor will disappear,

> "not in the sense that individuals will sink into indolent inactivity, but that their productive activities will take on the character of free creative self-expression not performed for wages or acquisitive purposes. Productive activity, having undergone 'Aufhebung' as labor, will continue in a new mode".[1]

---

1 R.C. Tucker, op. cit., p. xlii.

The communist revolution does not only liberate the proletariat from oppression, exploitation and dependence. It liberates the capitalist from capitalism and humanity from necessity. The end of labor in the sense of toil is possible because science and technology have enhanced productivity. Freedom is achieved through knowledge of nature and its laws and the application of this knowledge in technology and production. Science is a weapon in man's struggle against nature and for freedom.

> "[T]hat it is only possible to achieve real liberation in the real world and by employing real means, that slavery cannot be abolished without the steam engine and the mule and spinning-jenny, serfdom cannot be abolished without improved agriculture, and that, in general, people cannot be liberated as long as they are unable to obtain food and drink, housing and clothing in adequate quality and quantity. 'Liberation' is a historical and not a mental act, and it is brought about by historical conditions, the [development] of industry, commerce, [agri]culture".[1]

> "[T]he young Marx became convinced that the reason why the French Revolution had failed to found freedom was that it had failed to solve the social question. From this he concluded that freedom and poverty were incompatible. His most explosive and indeed most original contribution to the cause of revolution was that he interpreted the compelling needs of mass poverty in political terms as an uprising, not for the sake of bread or wealth, but for the sake of freedom as well".[2]

The different stages of historical development are characterized by the degree of control over the forces of nature. Every major development of the means of production is a step forward in the liberation from nature and the inauguration of a next stage in the historical development of society. Agriculture for example meant more control because less dependence on the seasons. And the extraordinary development of

---

1 K. Marx, *The German Ideology*, in R.C. Tucker, op. cit., p. 169.
2 H. Arendt, *On Revolution*, op. cit., p. 62.

tools and machines during the industrial revolution increased productivity to such an extent that complete freedom from nature and necessity is now possible.

Capitalism, characterized by industrialization, has been one step further forward in this process and is therefore a necessary step towards the full liberation of mankind. Communism, the last step, cannot come about in a society which has not yet taken the step towards capitalism because pre-capitalist societies have not yet acquired the means of production necessary for freedom from nature. "In broad outlines Asiatic, ancient, feudal, and modern bourgeois modes of production can be designated as progressive epochs in the economic formation of society".[1]

History is a process of continuous liberation. In capitalism, the most developed form of society until now, the ultimate liberation has become a real possibility. Because of high levels of productivity and mechanization, man can be freed from nature altogether.

The power of man over nature, and hence his liberty, depends on the powers of nature. These powers of nature have to be known and applied for the purposes of man. Mythology is an inadequate knowledge of nature and is typical of societies with an inadequate control over nature. Developed forces of production require a developed knowledge of nature. "[T]he low economic development of the prehistoric period is supplemented and also partially conditioned and even caused by the false conceptions of nature".[2]

A better knowledge of nature means more control over nature. Freedom is therefore a conscious necessity. Knowledge of necessity and of the laws of nature, and the application of this knowledge, can produce freedom. Freedom is

---

1 K. Marx, *Preface to A Contribution to the Critique of Political Economy*, in R.C. Tucker, op. cit., p. 5.

2 F. Engels, *Letter to J. Bloch (1890)*, in R.C. Tucker, op. cit., p. 763.

understanding of necessity, not some kind of impossible independence from necessity. Knowing the laws of nature does not make us independent from them, but gives us the possibility to use them for our purposes.[1]

This means that there will be necessity even in the realm of freedom. Freedom can only exist within necessity. Nature and its laws will always exist. Freedom does not mean that nature disappears. It only means that we use nature in such a way that it works for us instead of against us. We will always have to struggle against nature, but in the realm of freedom this struggle will be more relaxed and with a minimum expenditure of energy.

> "Just as the savage must wrestle with Nature to satisfy his wants, to maintain and reproduce life, so must civilized man, and he must do so in all social formations and under all possible modes of production. With his development this realm of physical necessity expands as a result of his wants; but, at the same time, the forces of production which satisfy these wants also increase. Freedom in this field can only consist in interchange with Nature, bringing it under their common control, instead of being ruled by it as by the blind forces of Nature; and achieving this with the least expenditure of energy and under conditions most favorable to, and worthy of, their human nature. But it nonetheless still remains a realm of necessity. Beyond it begins that development of human energy which is an end in itself, the true realm of freedom, which, however, can blossom forth only with the realm of necessity as its basis. The shortening of the working day is its basic prerequisite".[2]

Labor and Wage

However, nature is not the only oppressor. Technology and industry are not enough for real liberation. Capitalism is a necessary step towards communism and a huge progress

---

1 F. Engels, *Anti-Dühring*, op. cit., p. 312.

2 K. Marx, *Das Kapital*, in F. Fukuyama, op. cit., p. 132.

compared to previous steps. But it is not enough. It delivers the means to liberate men from nature but not from each other. The rule of man over man eliminates the possibility of freedom from nature. The hugely productive means of production are not used to liberate but to enslave and drive the workers into poverty.

Capitalism enslaves and inhibits free individual development, free creative production and self-expression, not only because of immiserization, but also because it reduces labor to a merchandise, something you buy in order to accumulate surplus value and to get rich, or something you sell in order to survive. In spite of the enormous technological advances, labor remains a means to material survival rather than productive self-expression and self-realization. People go to work, not to produce but to survive. "[M]aterial life appears as the end, and what produces this material life, labor (which is now the only possible but, as we see, negative form of self-activity), as the means".[1]

> "All our invention and progress seem to result in endowing material forces with intellectual life, and in stultifying human life into a material force. This antagonism between modern industry and science on the one hand, modern misery and dissolution on the other hand; this antagonism between the productive forces, and the social relations of our epoch is a fact, palpable, overwhelming, and not to be controverted".[2]

People work in order to live, and not in order to produce or to develop or express themselves through production. Labor is a burden, not a free activity. Instead of developing his possibilities and talents through work, the worker stultifies them. The purpose of his activity is not the product — he does not care and often does not even know what he produces

---

1 K. Marx, *The German Ideology*, in R.C. Tucker, op. cit., p. 191.

2 K. Marx, *Speech at the Anniversary of the People's Paper*, in R.C. Tucker, op. cit., p. 578.

— but his wage. His labor is not the expression of his life; his life starts after work.

> "[T]he product of his activity is not the object of his activity. What he produces for himself is not the silk that he weaves, not the gold that he draws from the mine, not the palace that he builds. What he produces for himself is wages, and silk, gold, palace resolve themselves for him into a definite quantity of the means of subsistence, perhaps into a cotton jacket, some copper coins and a lodging in a cellar. And the worker, who for twelve hours weaves, spins, drills, turns, builds, shovels, breaks stones, carries loads, etc. — does he consider this twelve hours' weaving, spinning, drilling, turning, building, shoveling, stone-breaking as a manifestation of his life, as life? On the contrary, life begins for him where this activity ceases, at table, in the public house, in bed. The twelve hours' labor, on the other hand, has no meaning for him as weaving, spinning, drilling, etc., but as earnings, which bring him to the table, to the public house, into bed".[1]

New Labor (1)

Labor, rather than a burden or a matter of indifference to the worker, must become self-expression, self-development and self-creation, a spontaneous and freely chosen production of things that shape and externalize the identity of the worker. But this can only happen when workers can choose and organize their activity themselves. This means that workers must associate and decide their organization and goals. And this in turn presupposes a social organization in which the means of production are freely available for everyone. "[I]n the appropriation by the proletarians, a mass of instruments of production must be made subject to each individual, and property to all".[2]

---

1 K. Marx, *Wage Labor and Capital*, in D. McLellan, *The Thought of Karl Marx*, op. cit., p. 168-169.

2 K. Marx, *The German Ideology*, in R.C. Tucker, op. cit., p. 191.

The goal of communism is not merely higher wages or better labor conditions (as demanded by social-democrats for instance) but a radical transformation of labor, away from an alienated activity that merely produces survival and surplus value. Survival, wage or surplus value should not be the goal of labor, not even decent survival, high wages or minimal surplus value. A higher wage or a minimal surplus value only means that the system of labor as a commodity continues to exist. Labor should serve self-creation and self-expression. Higher wages and better labor conditions do not change the fundamental structure of a society characterized by private ownership of the means of production.

> "For us the issue cannot be the alteration of private property but only its annihilation, not the smoothing over of class antagonisms but the abolition of classes, not the improvement of existing society but the foundation of a new one".[1]

Only a fundamental modification of the structure of ownership in society can produce an ideal kind of labor. The separation between owners of the means of production and non-owners must be abolished and the means of production must be handed over to society. If the means of production do not belong to society, then there will always be some people who own them and some who don't. The latter are dependent and cannot engage in free creative activity because they cannot choose the means for this activity. They have to sell their labor power, which is all they have. The purpose of labor then becomes their wage rather than the product of their labor. Communism demands "the appropriation of the means of production, their subjection to the associated working class and, therefore, the abolition of wage labor as well as of capital

---

1 Marx, Engels, *Address of the Central Committee to the Communist League*, in R.C. Tucker, op. cit., p. 505.

and of their mutual relations".[1] This indeed is such a fundamental transformation of society that a revolution is necessary. The owners will not peacefully accept expropriation.

Communism believes that modern production does not and should not require a wage-system and a separation between employers and employees.

> "Production on a large scale, and in accord with the behest of modern science, may be carried on without the existence of a class of masters employing a class of hands; ... to bear fruit, the means of labor need not be monopolized as a means of dominion over, and of extortion against, the laboring man himself; and ... like slave labor, like serf labor, hired labor is but a transitory and inferior form, destined to disappear before associated labor plying its toil with a willing hand, a ready mind, and a joyous heart".[2]

Communism also refuses to accept social security as it exists today in many developed countries. Unemployment benefits, wage agreements, labor condition regulations, etc. may help people to avoid poverty and correct the capitalist tendency for exploitation, but they cannot give people a meaningful activity, let alone self-creation and self-development. The absence of labor activity, even if it is compensated by unemployment benefits, is just as bad as labor with the only purpose to earn a wage and to survive. Which is worse: forced albeit paid inactivity, or being considered as a merchandise, a container for labor power, an object, a part of a machine?

Labor must become an activity which does not only serve the animal side of man but also his human side, not only survival but also self-improvement, not only a means for what happens afterwards but a goal in itself. It should be a joy rather than a burden.

---

1 F. Engels, *Introduction to The Class Struggles in France (Marx)*, in R.C. Tucker, op. cit., p. 559.

2 K. Marx, *Inaugural Address of the Working Men's International Association*, in R.C. Tucker, op. cit., p. 518.

Division of Labor

Capitalist labor must be abolished because it reduces labor to a means of survival (easy or difficult survival depending on the success of social corrections to the system), because it does not allow the associated workers to use the means of production in a creative and spontaneous way, but also because it forces workers into a rigid system of division of labor. This system, like the wage system and the private ownership of the means of production, inhibits self-development.

Technology and the automation of labor increase productivity, which is positive, but also increase specialization. The worker becomes a detail-worker who executes very limited tasks, or perhaps even one task, because in modern industry every task is isolated, taken apart and divided into its most elementary parts. The production process has become so complex that one man can no longer master it from start to finish, physically or intellectually. Labor becomes monotonous, mechanical, one-sided and repetitive.

The division of labor makes it impossible for the worker to produce anything and therefore destroys creativity, self-expression and self-development. It is the system that produces, and the worker is only a tiny part in this system, often unaware of the nature, composition and overall fabrication process of the final product. Perhaps he doesn't even know what the people before and after him are doing. He cannot develop his "natural human urge toward spontaneous productive activity".[1] Rather than his will or his purposefulness, he develops only one tiny activity which in itself is rather meaningless and without a product. He becomes stupid and often even sacrifices his health as a result of monotony and indifference.

---

1 R.C. Tucker, op. cit., p. xxxi.

"This stunting of man grows in the same measure as the division of labor, which attains its highest development in manufacture. Manufacture splits up each trade into its separate partial operations, allots each of these to an individual laborer as his life calling, and thus chains him for life to a particular detail function and a particular tool. 'It converts the laborer into a crippled monstrosity, by forcing his detail dexterity at the expense of a world of productive capabilities and instincts ... The individual himself is made the automatic motor of a fractional operation' (Marx, Capital) — a motor which in many cases is perfected only by literally crippling the laborer physically and mentally. The machinery of modern industry degrades the laborer from a machine to the mere appendage of a machine. 'The life-long speciality of handling one and the same tool, now becomes the lifelong speciality of serving one and the same machine. Machinery is put to a wrong use, with the object of transforming the workman, from his very childhood, into a part of a detail-machine' (Marx, Capital)".[1]

The worker is a replaceable part of an enormous organization, of a meta-machine containing both machines and humans. He is replaceable because his task is so detailed and stripped of complexity for the sake of easy and fast processing, that it can be taken over by any other worker or by a new machine. He is like an organ in a huge organism and in an age of routine transplants.

In such a system, labor cannot be used to be creative or to form and express an identity through production. The creation of products is an essential part in the creation and expression of identity, but the modern worker does not create products. The system or organization creates products and the worker only contributes an insignificant part. He may be totally unaware of the final product and of the other parts contributed by his colleagues.

---

1 F. Engels, *On the Division of Labor in Production, Anti-Dühring*, in R.C. Tucker, op. cit., p. 719.

The activity of the worker does not have a goal. It's merely a means in a larger goal. Because he is often unaware of what came before, what comes after and what is the ultimate product of it all, his activity seems purposeless to him, although in reality it has a small purpose. A man without a purpose and without understanding of what is going on, is not a man. How can the worker see his work as an integral part of his life? Work is therefore again something which merely serves survival; life starts after work.

Division of labor also implies the power of the organizer. The capitalist, the owner of the production system, is the only one who oversees, understands and controls everything. Division of labor requires hierarchical organization, the authoritarian imposition of strict rules that have to be rigorously enforced if the system is to operate. There is no freedom at all. The capitalist isn't free either because technology forces him to impose a strict organization which he is not free to choose. Science and competition impose the most efficient form of organization.

The positive fact of cooperation turns into something negative, namely the isolation of the worker and his separation from the overall production process.[1] Division of labor, automation or organization increase productivity but the worker suffers in the process.

> "[W]ithin the capitalist system all methods for raising the social productiveness of labor are brought about at the cost of the individual laborer; all means for the development of production transform themselves into means of domination over, and exploitation of, the producers; they mutilate the laborer into a fragment of a man, degrade him to the level of an appendage of a machine, destroy every remnant of charm in his work and turn it into a hated toil; they estrange from him the intellectual potentialities of the labor-process in the same proportion as science is incorporated in it as an

---

1 F. Chatelet, op. cit., p. 57.

> independent power; they distort the conditions under which he works, subject him during the labor-process to a despotism the more hateful for its meanness; they transform his life-time into working-time, and drag his wife and child beneath the wheels of the Juggernaut of capital".[1]

However, as we will see below, the fact that modern production requires high levels of cooperation and organization, is a prerequisite for the eventual organization of the proletariat and its transformation into a political force.

New Labor (2)

Communism demands a new and more human organization of labor and production, without wage or division of labor. Productivity is enhanced by division of labor, but even more by a system that allows all producers to develop all their possibilities and talents.

> "[I]n time to come there will no longer be any professional porters or architects, ... the man who for half an hour gives instructions as an architect will also push a barrow for a period, until his activity as an architect is once again required. It is a fine sort of socialism which perpetuates the professional porter!"[2]

> "In a communist society there are no painters but at most people who engage in painting among other activities".[3]

> "In communist society, where nobody has one exclusive sphere of activity but each can become accomplished in any branch he wishes, society regulates the general production and thus makes it possible for me to do one thing today and another tomorrow, to hunt in the morning, fish in the afternoon, rear cattle in the evening, criticize after dinner, just as I have a mind, without ever becoming hunter, fisherman, shepherd

1 K. Marx, *Capital*, op. cit., p. 359-360.

2 F. Engels, *On the Division of Labor in Production, Anti-Dühring*, in R.C. Tucker, op. cit., p. 718.

3 K. Marx, *The German Ideology*, in D. McLellan, *The Thought of Karl Marx*, op. cit., p. 247.

or critic. This fixation of social activity, this consolidation of what we ourselves produce into an objective power above us, growing out of our control, thwarting our expectations, bringing to naught our calculations, is one of the chief factors in historical development up till now".[1]

"[P]roductive labor, instead of being a means of subjugating men, will become a means of their emancipation, by offering each individual the opportunity to develop all his faculties, physical and mental, in all directions and exercise them to the full — in which, therefore, productive labor will become a pleasure instead of being a burden".[2]

Communist production abolishes the life-long connection to a single and simple task, just as it abolishes wage labor. The latter is done by way of the expropriation and socialization of the means of production. The former as well, but requires also further automation, replacing the quasi-automatic human activity.

"In the Grundrisse Marx implied that the whole problem of the division of labor would be by-passed by the introduction of automated machinery and the drastic reduction in the working day: the problem then would no longer be labor but how to use leisure time".[3]

The socialization of the means of production will also counteract division of labor because it allows workers to go with ease from one activity to another. In capitalism, it is much more difficult to leave one factory or one task for another. Liberated from wage, dependence and division of labor, workers will be able to choose their own goals and means and to undertake a variety of activities that are goals rather than just means for survival. They will do so in association which

1 K. Marx, *The German Ideology*, in R.C. Tucker, op. cit., p. 160.

2 F. Engels, *On the Division of Labor in Production, Anti-Dühring*, in R.C. Tucker, op. cit., p. 721.

3 D. McLellan, *Marx*, op. cit., p. 68.

each other because the means of production are under their common control. Communism is

> "the free activity of human beings producing in co-operative association. The socialization of the means of production was not, on this view, the essence of socialism or communism, but only its precondition".[1]

> "Marx's term for the new mode of production which he envisages arising on the yonder side of history, after the world-wide proletarian revolution, is 'associated' production".[2]

Both wage labor and division of labor alienate the worker from the product of his labor. Division of labor means that the product of labor is not the product of the laborer. The product of his labor is something alien to him. It does not belong to him, it is not his product. It is the product of the organization. In the case of wage-labor it is the product of the capitalist. The product of a worker's labor is his wage, and division of labor puts the tangible product of his activity so far away, and shrinks his input so much that the result can be altogether unknown. Even the function of his tiny contribution can be a mystery.

Labor is something outside of the worker, not part of his real life, not his own, spontaneous activity. Labor has no sense apart from survival. The worker, even if he wanted, could not work for a product rather than for his survival because his product is unknown to him and he does not even care about this because his wage is all that counts. He works for his survival, not for a product, for his personal development or creativity. And he is forced to think and act like this because he has to work in a system in which others decide on the use of the means of production, and decide that division of labor is the best way to use these means.

---

1 R.C. Tucker, op. cit., p. xxxi-xxxii.
2 Ibid., p. xlii.

Communism will abolish alienation and labor for the purpose of survival. It will put an end to oppression of man by man, caused by private property of the means of production which has led to wage labor, dependence, expropriation of surplus value, division of labor and the oppressive state structure that is necessary to maintain all this.

Communism, in order to liberate man, must liberate him from nature and fellow-man. This is said to be possible by way of the socialization of the means of production. Socialization will enhance productivity (because production will be organized in such a way that all talents of all workers are developed and used) and hence liberate man completely from nature. It will also liberate man from his fellow-man because the latter is no longer able to monopolize the means of production and to exploit the workers. He can no longer expropriate surplus value or force workers to work for a wage rather than for a product and for their own development. And, finally, the socialization of the means of production will make it possible to undo the rigid division of labor and its dulling effects.

This socialization means that society as a whole takes control over the means of production. Only then can workers go from one activity to another and develop all their possibilities. The anarchy in the current production system is replaced by planned organization.[1] "[M]en get exchange, production, the mode of their mutual relation, under their own control again".[2]

---

[1] F. Engels, *Anti-Dühring*, op. cit., p. 446.
[2] K. Marx, *The German Ideology*, in R.C. Tucker, op. cit., p. 162.

Figure 5: Old Labor

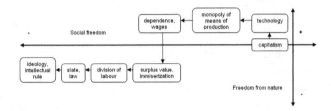

Figure 6: New Labor

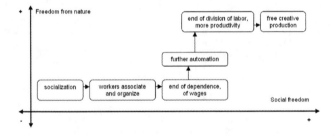

CHAPTER 3. AUTONOMOUS DEVELOPMENT

Historical Materialism

Prehistory is not over. Our current time is not real history, it is still prehistory. History will start with communism. But prehistory is not irrational, mythological, chaotic, barbaric or stupid. There is development and progress in prehistory, a movement towards a definite goal. It has a plan and a direction. It is a whole.

The movement of society or the succession of stages of development of society, is automatic and necessary. One stage necessarily and automatically goes over into another one, and each one is an advance compared to the previous one. Marx claimed to have discovered the laws of the development of society, from its lower forms to its higher forms. "[T]he birth, life and death of a given social organism and its replacement by another, superior order".[1]

---

1 K. Marx, in D. McLellan, *Marx*, op. cit., p. 51.

Communism claims to be able to predict the future development of social forms. On the basis of the forces and laws that were at work in the past and still are in the present, and that determined the passage of one form of society to another, communism predicts the future and ultimate passage to a new society, the beginning of history.

However, what are these forces? What causes social change, the replacement of one period by another and the movement and direction of society as a whole? Certainly material rather than intellectual forces, economic rather than political, moral or religious ones. The forces of production, the relations of production and the struggles between classes rather than ideals or theories drives history forwards.

> "Saint Bruno even goes so far as to assert that 'only criticism and critics have made history' ... If these theorists treat really historical subjects, as for instance the eighteenth century, they merely give a history of the ideas of the times, torn away from the facts and the practical development fundamental to them".[1] "[T]he real production of life seems to be primeval history, while the truly historical appears to be separated from ordinary life, something extra-superterrestrial. With this the relation of man to nature is excluded from history and hence the antithesis of nature and history is created. The exponents of this conception of history have consequently only been able to see in history the political actions of princes and States, religious and all sorts of theoretical struggles, and in particular in each historical epoch have had to share the illusion of that epoch. For instance, if an epoch imagines itself to be actuated by purely 'political' or 'religious' motives, although 'religion' and 'politics' are only forms of its true motives, the historian accepts this opinion. The 'idea', the 'conception' of the people in question about their real practice, is transformed into the sole determining, active force, which controls and determines their practice".[2]

1 K. Marx, *The German Ideology*, in R.C. Tucker, op. cit., p. 167.
2 Ibid., p. 165.

Just as we cannot judge individuals according to the ideas they have of themselves, we cannot do so for epochs. Communism wants to explain "theoretical talk from the actual existing conditions"[1] and do away with the opinion that "history is always under the sway of ideas",[2] an opinion which can only exist once people start to distinguish between material and mental labor. Not the thinkers make history or force society to go from one period to the next, but the forces and modes of production, and the resulting class relationships:

> "[T]he hand mill will give you a society with the feudal lord, the steam mill a society with the industrial capitalist".[3] "[T]he multitude of productive forces accessible to men determines the nature of society, hence, ... the 'history of humanity' must always be studied and treated in relation to the history of industry and exchange".[4]

A phase in human history, the existence of society in a specific form, is determined by the presence of certain forces of production and the resulting relations of production.

> "The relations of production in their totality constitute what are called the social relations, society, and, specifically, a society at a definite stage of historical development, a society with a peculiar, distinctive character. Ancient society, feudal society, bourgeois society are such totalities of production relations, each of which at the same time denotes a special stage of development in the history of mankind".[5] "[T]he essential element in an understanding of man and his history [is] a comprehension of man's productive activity".[6] "Men have history because they must produce their life, and because they must produce it moreover in a certain way".[7]

---

1 Ibid., p. 166.

2 Ibid., p. 174.

3 K. Marx, in D. McLellan, *The Thought of Karl Marx*, op. cit., p. 137.

4 K. Marx, *The German Ideology*, in R.C. Tucker, op. cit., p. 157.

5 K. Marx, *Wage Labor and Capital*, in D. McLellan, *The Thought of Karl Marx*, op. cit., p. 143.

6 D. McLellan, *Marx*, op. cit., p. 38.

7 K. Marx, *The German Ideology*, in R.C. Tucker, op. cit., p. 158.

Between the Imposed and the Fabricated

The laws of history are laws of evolution, of the passage of one epoch to the next, not laws which imply some kind of invariability of human society or behavior (as the laws which are sometimes "discovered" by conservatives). The final goal of historical development will come with the force of a law of nature, and is therefore independent from human intervention and automatic. But people can help the development along, or can hinder it, voluntarily or involuntarily, because people are not always conscious of the flow of history.

The fabrication of the Good Society is not impossible in communism. Social engineering is combined with a theory of the laws of historical development. The first and most important cause of a social revolution is not a theory or a plan that is then applied to society like an engineer may apply his plan to his material. The causes are modifications in the modes of production. These modifications and their impact on society, empirically analyzed and distilled into laws, determine the flow of history. Individuals go along with this flow. They don't decide it.

But people can play the role of the midwife of history. The child will be born anyway, whether one wants it or not, but certain actions can facilitate or fasten the birth. History can be lent a hand. Which actions, we will see later, but Marx is infamous for his statement that violence can be the midwife of an old society pregnant with a new one.

The rationality of history does not mean that men should be passive. But only those actions which fit into the flow of history and do not go against it, can be successful (like in the case of the laws of nature, as we have seen). Actions should promote the inevitable events. All other actions are irrational and ultimately unsuccessful as well. It is useless "to attempt with fragile human hands to steer the colossal ship of society against the natural currents and storms of history".[1] Trying to stop the impending changes is like trying to stop the law of gravity. Economic development is inexorable.

Community Destroys Capitalism

Before we discuss the margin of action, first a few words on the reasons why the transformation of capitalist society into communism is said to be inevitable, a historical necessity. The capitalist, or the bourgeoisie, creates a proletariat, a class which owns no means of production, is dependent and will become increasingly poor. This is inevitable. Capitalists need a class which is willing to sell its labor power, therefore a class which does not have its own means of production. Afterwards, they are forced to maximize surplus value and therefore make the workers poor. Competition between capitalists compels them to lower wages, enhance productivity, make the working day longer, and maximize surplus value. The capitalist "is incompetent to assure an existence to [his] slave within his slavery".[2] As a result, he creates a class of people who have nothing to lose. And those are always the most dangerous people.

The bourgeoisie produces its own gravediggers. The proletariat is forced to unite and organize into a class in order to resist the downward spiral created by capitalism, and is bound to become a force which will destroy private property, the original cause of all its misery. This growth of community feeling is enhanced by the very specific nature of the modern capitalist and industrial mode of production. Highly orga-

---

1 K. Popper, *The Open Society and its Enemies*, Routledge, London, 1995, p. 316.
2 Marx, Engels, *The Communist Manifesto*, op. cit., p. 93.

nized production in large factories operated by large groups of people, often close to large working-class neighborhoods, require combined, co-operative and community labor.[1]

This rise of community feeling is caused by the technological progress of the forces of production, which first causes modifications in the modes of production (division of labor, production on a larger scale thanks to machinery, increased co-operation between large numbers of people, etc.), and then causes community consciousness of the proletariat.

The original advances in technology made the rest inevitable. Once there are machines, factories automatically become bigger. Large scale production also yields competitive advantages because of increased productivity and lower per unit labor costs compared to individual production. More can be made with a lesser cost, and hence a lower price, which inevitably pulls people to these products and hence also to these modes of production. Because of the competitive advantage of the bigger producers, they will automatically swallow up the smaller ones, which causes capitalism.

Hence, more and more workers are active in big industrial factories. As a result, workers become organized and ultimately become so strong that they can overthrow capitalism.

The organized proletariat will not, however, destroy the original technological causes of capitalism. Communism will use the same technology. It will only destroy the private ownership of the technological means of production and the resulting relations of production. This ownership, as we have seen, is more and more concentrated in the hands of a few capitalists because of the technological necessity to produce in a few large factories rather than in many individual workshops, and because of the competitive advantages of these factories which eliminate smaller producers.

---

1 F. Engels, *Anti-Dühring*, op. cit., p. 436-437.

The technological advances and the productivity gains of capitalist production will be maintained in communism, but only organized in a different way, without private ownership. Anyway, private ownership of huge, community based forces of production is an anachronism. It's a remnant of feudalism.

Figure 7: Inevitable Revolt

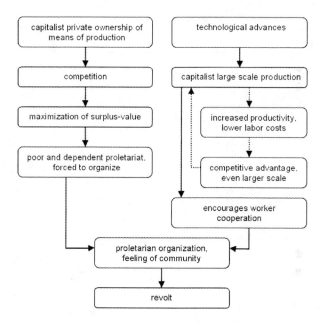

The modern forces of production and the proletariat are the two weapons, involuntarily forged by the bourgeoisie to bring death to itself.[1]

> "Along with the constantly diminishing number of the magnates of capital ... grows the mass of misery, oppression, slavery, degradation, exploitation; but with this too grows the revolt of the working class, a class always increasing in numbers, and disciplined, united,

---

1 Marx, Engels, *The Communist Manifesto*, op. cit., p. 87.

organized by the very mechanism of the process of capitalist production itself".[1]

Capitalism is the agent of its own destruction. The proletariat only executes the sentence that capitalism has passed on itself.

Big Industry Destroys Private Property

The growing feeling of community inside and between factories turns capitalistic private property into an anachronism and makes the socialization of the means of production the only realistic option. The bourgeois relations of production and the connected relations of property (the latter are but the legal expression of the former) are no longer in sync with the forces of production and have to adapt.[2] This is necessary and inevitable.

When they do, the class struggle will be over because there will no longer be classes. There will be no more ruling class oppressing the rest of society because the means of production will be the equal property of all. The relations of production will be based on common property and will finally be in sync with modern production technology.

However, this synchronization will not happen quickly or smoothly. There are forces in favor of it (e.g., the development of community feeling), but also forces against, like the capitalists of course, but also some of the workers. Capitalism tries to divide the workers.

> "Competition separates individuals from one another, not only the bourgeois but still more the workers, in spite of the fact that it brings them together. Hence it is a long time before these individuals can unite, apart from the fact that for the purposes of this union — if it is not to be merely local — the necessary means, the

---

1 K. Marx, *Capital*, op. cit., p. 378.

2 K. Marx, *Preface to A Contribution to the Critique of Political Economy*, in R.C. Tucker, op. cit., p. 4.

great industrial cities and cheap and quick commu-
nications, have first to be produced by big industry.
Hence every organized power standing over against
these isolated individuals, who live in relationships
daily reproducing this isolation, can only be overcome
after long struggles. To demand the opposite would be
tantamount to demanding that competition should not
exist in this definite epoch of history, or that the individuals should banish from their minds relationships
over which in their isolation they have no control".[1]

Big industry causes "a striking contrast between the increasingly social character of the capitalist process of production and the anti-social character of capitalist private
property".[2]

"[I]n big industry the contradiction between the instrument of production and private property appears
for the first time and is the product of big industry;
moreover, big industry must be highly developed to
produce this contradiction. And thus only with big industry does the abolition of private property become
possible".[3]

The industrial mode of production, developed during the
bourgeois era, makes communism possible. Communism is
impossible before or without it. (This is stage 't' in figure 3
above). "The organization of revolutionary elements as a class
supposes the existence of all the productive forces which
could be engendered in the bosom of the old society".[4] Only
when the forces of production have been fully developed and
have outgrown the relations of property, and when all conservative forces have been vanquished can a new society arise.
But these conservative forces fight a losing battle anyway.
The forces of production introduce change with the force of

---

1 K. Marx, *The German Ideology*, in R.C. Tucker, op. cit., p. 186.

2 D. McLellan, *Marx*, op. cit., p. 57.

3 K. Marx, *The German Ideology*, in R.C. Tucker, op. cit., p. 189-190.

4 K. Marx, *The Poverty of Philosophy*, in R.C. Tucker, op. cit., p. 218.

nature. "[B]ourgeois industry and commerce create [the] material conditions of a new world".[1]

Preconditions for Communism

The claim that private property of the means of production should be abolished does not make communism what it is. Other, pre-communist theories had already the same ideal. Communism is original because it claims that this ideal is only possible when certain material preconditions are present, and that, given their presence, communism is not only possible but inevitable.

Aspirations or desires are not preconditions, although they will help because worker consciousness, created by the industrial mode of production, is also a force for change. But ultimately, the economy is what counts, and, more specifically, a certain stage in the development of economic production.

> "A radical revolution is tied to certain historical conditions of economic development; these are its prerequisites. It is therefore only possible where, with capitalist production, the industrial proletariat occupies at least a significant position among the mass of the people ... But there the innermost thought of Mr Bakunin comes to light. He does not understand a thing about social revolution, only the political phrases about it; its economic conditions do not exist for him. Now since all hitherto existing economic forms, developed or undeveloped, include the servitude of the worker (be it in the form of the wage worker, peasant, etc.) he believes that in all of them a radical revolution is equally possible. But even more ! He wants the European social revolution, founded on the economic basis of capitalist production, to take place at the level of the Russian or Slav agricultural and pastoral people ... Will, not economic conditions, is the foundation of his social revolution".[2]
> "Marx was always scathing about those he referred to

---

1 K. Marx, *The Results of British Rule in India*, in D. McLellan, *The Thought of Karl Marx*, op. cit., p. 234.

2 K. Marx, *Marx on Bakunin (1875)*, in D. McLellan, *The Thought of Karl Marx*, op. cit., p. 238.

as 'the alchemists of revolution' who tried to provoke revolt whatever the socio-economic circumstances".[1]

This does not mean that communism will remain a privilege for industrial societies in the West. On the contrary, communism will be global according to communists. But then capitalism first has to become global.

> "[Marx] talked of the Asiatic mode of production, but did not integrate it into his scheme of historical development. According to him this mode of production was static and destined to be overtaken by the spread of capitalism over the whole globe".[2]

Of course, the most advanced capitalist countries, mainly in the West, will be first and will be the catalyst and initiator for the global revolution. "Europe's advanced capitalism made it appear the natural epicentre of world revolution".[3] "Once Europe is reorganized, and North America, that will furnish such colossal power and such an example that the semi-civilized countries will of themselves follow in their wake".[4]

The Solution is in the Problem

The capitalist mode of production contains the seeds of its own destruction. Capitalism is therefore progressive, it is aimed at the future, although individual capitalists are naturally conservative. It is a step on the way to communism. It paves the way. "[C]apitalism [is] ... destructive and inhuman but at the same time regenerative in that [it lays] ... the foundations for a new form of society".[5] The new breaks through the cracks in the old. The solution does not come from the outside but is contained in the problem. "[C]ommunist society, not as it has developed on its own foundations, but, on

---

1 D. McLellan, *Marx*, op. cit., p. 62.

2 Ibid., p. 83.

3 R.C. Tucker, op. cit., p. 676.

4 F. Engels, *Letter to K. Kautsky (1882)*, in R.C. Tucker, op. cit., p. 677.

5 D. McLellan, *Marx*, op. cit., p. 83.

the contrary, just as it emerges from capitalist society".[1] The material conditions and foundations for the new society grow in the old one.

> "No social order ever perishes before all the productive forces for which there is room in it have developed; and new, higher relations of production never appear before the material conditions of their existence have matured in the womb of the old society itself".[2]

The Revolution as Explosion

The continuing development of the production forces puts more and more pressure on the existing and non-evolving bourgeois property and production relations. Their self-interest tells the capitalists to try to maintain these relations using all possible means, including ideology, law, violence, and politics. But of course this only increases the tensions until the moment that there is a discharge and an explosion to release the tension.

This explosion is the revolutionary destruction of the capitalist relations of production and the creation of communist relations, under pressure of the developing forces of production. This revolution is inevitable and will inaugurate the recognition of the communal character of modern production. It will, in other words, destroy the outdated models of property adopted by capitalism. Private property will become common property, and will be in line with common production.

The passage from capitalism to communism is necessarily revolutionary because a natural development is held up artificially.

> "Centralization of the means of production and socialization of labor at last reach a point where they become incompatible with their capitalist integument.

---

1 K. Marx, *Critique of the Gotha Program*, in R.C. Tucker, op. cit., p. 529.

2 K. Marx, *Preface to A Contribution to the Critique of Political Economy*, in R.C. Tucker, op. cit., p. 5.

> This integument is burst asunder. The knell of capitalist private property sounds. The expropriators are expropriated".[1]

When exactly this burst will occur is obviously much more difficult to predict. And it is fair to say that we are still waiting.

The victorious revolution of the proletariat does not and should not make it the new master of the final form of society,

> "for it wins victory only by abolishing itself and its opposite. Both the proletariat itself and its conditioning opposite — private property — disappear with the victory of the proletariat. If socialist writers attribute this world-historical role to the proletariat, this is by no means ... because they regard the proletarians as gods. On the contrary. Since the fully formed proletariat represents, practically speaking, the complete abstraction from everything human, even from the appearance of being human; since all the living conditions of contemporary society have reached the acme of inhumanity in the living conditions of the proletariat; since in the proletariat man has lost himself, although at the same time he has both acquired a theoretical consciousness of this loss and has been directly forced into indignation against this inhumanity by virtue of an inexorable, utterly unembellishable, absolutely imperious need, that practical expression of necessity — because of all this the proletariat itself can and must liberate itself. But it cannot liberate itself without destroying its own living conditions. It cannot do so without destroying all the inhuman living conditions of contemporary society which are concentrated in its own situation. Not in vain does it go through the harsh but hardening school of labor. It is not a matter of what this or that proletarian or even the proletariat as a whole pictures at present as its goal. It is a matter of what the proletariat is in actuality and what, in accordance with this being, it will historically be compelled to do. Its goal and its historical action are prefigured in the most clear and ineluctable way in its own life-situation as well as in the whole organization of contemporary bourgeois society".[2]

---

1 K. Marx, *Capital*, op. cit., p. 378.
2 Marx, Engels, *The Holy Family*, in R.C. Tucker, op. cit., p. 134-135.

CHAPTER 4. HUMAN INTERVENTION

Helping the Inevitable

The autonomous development does not exclude human intervention and activism. A society which has discovered the laws of its development cannot ignore these laws but it can ease the pain of birth of the new society. We should not surrender slavishly to higher forces, cross our arms and sit back. We can be active and history will force us to be active in a certain way. "Activism can be justified only so long as it acquiesces in impending changes".[1]

We can change the world. "The philosophers have only interpreted the world, in various ways; the point, however, is to change it".[2] Communism is a kind of production or fabrication of society. A new society is created according to a pre-existing plan. A theory, communism, must be implemented, like a carpenter makes a table from a blueprint.

---

1 K. Popper, *The Poverty of Historicism*, op. cit., p. 51.
2 K. Marx, *Theses on Feuerbach*, in R.C. Tucker, op. cit., p. 145.

Human intervention is possible, because there is communist theory which tells us about the impending changes, about the nature of the society to be created and about the types of actions which will or will not help this creation. Revolutionaries will use this theory to justify and plan their actions, to organize and teach the proletariat so that they will rise up. The outcome is fixed, but we can fasten or delay it, make it more or less painful.

In a nutshell, the types of intervention recommended by communism are the following. Once the theory of communism is clearly stated, the workers must be informed about it and hence about the nature of their predicament and about the solution. The revolutionary proletariat, united, rebellious and organized not only by their predicament and by the nature of the productive forces but also by the agitation and expertise of professional communists, takes over the power of the state and transforms the state into a revolutionary workers' state. The state, now a means of power in the hands of the proletariat rather than the bourgeoisie, takes over control of production. It centralizes the forces of production, expropriating the capitalists, and it starts a new, centrally planned and organized mode of production.

The state, or we can say society because the state is now in the hands of the great majority of the people, makes itself "the master of all the means of production to use them in accordance with a social plan".[1] The take-over of the state and the reorganization of production happen with the use of violence.

---

1 F. Engels, *On the Division of Labor in Production, Anti-Dühring*, in R.C. Tucker, op. cit., p. 720.

The Dictatorship of the Proletariat

The take-over of the state creates the dictatorship of the proletariat. This new class rule is a step on the way to the abolition of all class rule. This dictatorship is necessary to force the destruction of the old mode of production and ownership rules, and to create new ones. "Someday the worker must seize political power in order to build up the new organization of labor".[1]

The capitalists will of course rebel. They lose the means of production and control over the powers of the state, but they will not accept this without a fight. They are thrown to the ground by the revolution, but they are not without power yet. Therefore they have to be contained dictatorially.

> "[A]s long as the other classes, and in particular the capitalist class, still exist, as long as the proletariat is still struggling with it (because, with the proletariat's conquest of governmental power its enemies and the old organization of society have not yet disappeared), it must use coercive means, hence governmental means; it is still a class and the economic conditions on which the class struggle and the existence of classes depend, have not yet disappeared and must be removed by force, or transformed and their process of transformation speeded up by force".[2]

> "[I]f the victorious party does not want to have fought in vain, it must maintain this rule by means of the terror which its arms inspire in the reactionaries. Would the Paris Commune have lasted a single day if it had not made use of this authority of the armed people against the bourgeois? Should we not, on the contrary, reproach it for not having used it freely enough?".[3]

The revolution does not only depose the old rulers and take the state from their hands. The revolutionaries, tempo-

---

1 K. Marx, in R.C. Tucker, op. cit., p. 523.

2 K. Marx, *Marx on Bakunin*, in D. McLellan, *The Thought of Karl Marx*, op. cit., p. 237-238.

3 F. Engels, *On Authority*, in R.C. Tucker, op. cit., p. 733.

rarily, take the state into their own hands and use it to transform the system of production and suppress reactionaries in the process. If they don't act like this, their revolution will not survive. It will perish in what Marx called a new war of slave-owners, referring to the American civil war.

The dictatorship of the proletariat is temporary because it is only necessary to destroy the old society and create the new one. Old forms of ownership must be replaced by new ones, and resistance against this must be overcome. But when the new ones are in place, there's no reason anymore to have a state, and the dictatorship of the proletariat will cease. "The class domination of the workers over the resisting strata of the old world must last until the economic foundations of the existence of classes are destroyed".[1]

When destroying the capitalist relations of production, the ruling proletariat will destroy all classes and all class rule, including its own rule. because the new relations of production will no longer require classes. Communism uses the word "dictatorship" in its Roman meaning which stressed its temporary nature; "the Roman office of 'dictatura' where all power was legally concentrated in the hands of a single man during a limited period in a time of crises".[2]

Now why will the rule of the proletariat destroy all classes and class rule? Because all classes and the rule of one over the other are always based on the unequal ownership of the means of production. When ownership is common, there will be no more need to rule over the non-owners, and hence there will be no more need for state, law, politics, or ideology. During the transition period from capitalism to communism, the dictatorship of the proletariat will be the temporary class rule of the new owners over the previous owners, because the

---

1 K. Marx, *After the Revolution, Marx debates Bakunin*, in R.C. Tucker, op. cit., p. 547.

2 D. McLellan, *Marx*, op. cit., p. 70.

communist revolution initially means nothing more than the takeover of the state and of the means of production by the proletariat. When the last remnants of capitalism have given up and have entered the ranks of the proletariat, and when common ownership is firmly established, this last state-form can also disappear. Then there will no longer be classes or remnants of them and hence no need for a state.

The state, the instrument of class oppression par excellence, in all its forms, absolute monarchy, capitalist democracy and dictatorship of the proletariat, will wither away. When property is common, there are no classes or class rule, and hence no reason for oppression and an instrument of oppression. In place of the rule over people comes the administration of things. Production will have to be organized but not by a state. The associated workers will do so.

> "The abolition of the state only has a meaning for communists as a necessary result of the suppression of classes whose disappearance automatically entails the disappearance of the need for an organized power of one class for the suppression of another".[1]

Only through the combination of the proletarian revolution and the proletarian dictatorship can the classless communist society be created.

> "What I did that was new was to prove: 1) that the existence of classes is only bound up with particular historical phases in the development of production, 2) that the class struggle necessarily leads to the dictatorship of the proletariat, 3) that this dictatorship itself only constitutes the transition to the abolition of all classes and to a classless society".[2]

Since capitalism, in its advanced form, is only kept alive by political, legal and ideological means, it can be overthrown with these means. The state, with its laws and ideology, sup-

---

1 K. Marx, *Review of E. Girardin, Socialism and Taxes*, in D. McLellan, *The Thought of Karl Marx*, op. cit., p. 219.

2 K. Marx, *Letter to J. Weydemeyer (1852)*, in R.C. Tucker, op. cit., p. 220.

ports capitalism against the historical current, and hence the take-over of the state can bring it down. When the capitalists no longer have the means of the state, their resistance will be futile.[1]

Of course, the proletariat as such is too numerous to take over the state. It's leaders must do so in their name. Just as these leaders informed the proletariat about its predicament and its future, incited it to revolt and organized it when it did revolt, so they must take over the state on its behalf.

However, this dictatorship is a kind of democracy, more democratic than capitalist democracy. In the latter, the minority rules over the majority, in the former the majority of the people, the proletariat, rules by way of its leaders. Because in this "democratic dictatorship" of the proletariat a minority is suppressed by the majority, it is possible to predict that, compared to the capitalist oppression of the majority by the minority, this coercion will be simple, short and not so bloody. Communism will then appear rather quickly and will not witness any oppression of any kind because there will be no more classes.

> "[A]s soon as the goal of the proletarian movement, the abolition of classes, shall have been reached, the power of the state, whose function it is to keep the great majority of producers beneath the yoke of a small minority of exploiters, will disappear and governmental functions will be transformed into simple administrative functions".[2]

> "The working class, in the course of its development, will substitute for the old civil society an association which will exclude classes and their antagonism, and there will be no more political power properly so-called, since political power is precisely the official expression of antagonism in civil society".[3]

1 See also H. Arendt, *On Revolution*, op. cit., p. 62.

2 K. Marx, *The Alleged Splits in the International*, in D. McLellan, *The Thought of Karl Marx*, op. cit., p. 211.

3 K. Marx, *The Poverty of Philosophy*, in D. McLellan, ibid., p. 186.

Freedom and Necessity

The relationship between communist experts or leaders and the proletariat is similar to the one between scientists and technicians. The first discover the laws and teach them; the latter apply them. Communism, the realm of freedom, shall be reached when the people, instructed by the communists, know the laws of social development and apply them, [1] like technicians know the laws of nature and apply them to achieve freedom from nature.

Inevitability and necessity do not exclude freedom. The necessity of the laws of nature does not mean that we are at the mercy of these laws, powerless and passive. Knowledge of this necessity means that we can use it for our purposes and achieve freedom in necessity. And the same is true, according to communism, for the necessity of historical development. The laws of history are applied to achieve freedom in history.

Freedom is conscious and applied necessity. The necessary revolutionary passage from one society to another will only occur when the majority of the proletariat will be conscious of its situation because of increased oppression and communist teaching, when it will be organized thanks to the nature of the forces of production and thanks to the communist party, and when it will be made aware of the future organization of society by the nature of the forces of production and by communist teaching about the development of society. This consciousness turns the proletariat into a class for itself and not merely in itself.

---

1 F. Engels, *Anti-Dühring*, in *Marx-Engels Gesamtausgabe*, op. cit., p. 446.

Figure 8: Communist Action

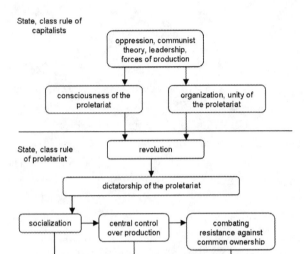

Education of the proletariat is very important in communism:

> "[I]n order that the masses may understand what is to be done, long, persistent work is required".[1] "The Communists ... are on the one hand, practically, the most advanced and resolute section of the working-class parties of every country, that section which pushes forward all others; on the other hand, theoretically, they have over the great mass of the proletariat the advantage of clearly understanding the line of march, the conditions, and the ultimate general results of the proletarian movement".[2] "One element of success they [the working classes] possess — numbers, but num-

1 F. Engels, *Introduction to The Class Struggles in France*, in R.C. Tucker, op. cit., p. 570.

2 Marx, Engels, *The Communist Manifesto*, op. cit., p. 95.

bers weigh only in the balance, if united by combination and led by knowledge".[1]

Since the state does not only rule with force but also with persuasion and influence, change cannot rely on force alone either, and has to be provoked by ideological means as well. A simple take-over of the state by the leaders of the communist party is useless if the workers are not yet conscious of the laws of history. A revolution must be preceded by a revolution in the minds. The workers must be made conscious of the illegitimacy of the current system and of their own historical role. Theory becomes a material force that changes the world, when the masses are instructed and led by professional communists.

Likewise, combating the resistance of the remnants of the old owners does not only mean the use of force to contain them but also re-education to convince them of the errors of their views.

Life and Death

History is the history of the productive forces and the relations of production. It is a process of birth, life and death of forms of society, each with its own temporary mode of production. The birth and death are determined by the evolution of the means of production. Capitalist society at the end of its evolution or its life is child-bearing. The new communist society is growing inside of it. Communism has its origin in the womb of capitalism. The future grows in the present. The old society is pregnant with the new one. And like in an accelerated version of Darwinism, every child is a higher form of its mother. "[T]he birth, life and death of a given social organism and its replacement by another, superior order".[2]

---

1 K. Marx, *Inaugural Address of the Working Men's International Association*, in R.C. Tucker, op. cit., p. 518.
2 K. Marx, in D. McLellan, *Marx*, op. cit., p. 51.

Of course, every birth is accompanied with labor. Revolution and the dictatorship of the proletariat represent the process of birth and the pain that it entails. The communists and the proletariat are the midwifes and their student-nurses respectively, each with their own level of knowledge of the theory of birth and social reproduction. They make the process of birth easier, smoother and shorter.

> "When a society has discovered the natural law that determines its own movement, even then it can neither overleap the natural phases of its evolution, nor shuffle them out of the world by a stroke of the pen. But this much it can do : it can shorten and lessen the birth-pangs".[1]

The mother dies in the bed of birth because the fetus has grown too much. The new society is born because the womb of the old one limits its further growth. The child "[will] be stamped with the birthmarks of the old society from whose womb it emerges".[2] So we will get for some time a new class rule, the dictatorship of the proletariat. Only after some time will the child lose these marks and will it no longer refer to its mother. This child is the last child. It will grow up to perfection and live forever.

The determinism and necessity of the historical evolution of society, implicit in the metaphor of birth, sits besides the activism and fabrication of the new society represented by the metaphor of the midwife. Every activity is based on the realization and facilitation of the movement of history. Politics must adapt to and is the slave of the laws of historical development. The theoretical prediction of the future produces the correct practical political actions which are so designed that they help and soften the inevitable realization of the predic-

1 K. Marx, *Capital*, in K. Popper, *The Poverty of Historicism*, op. cit., p. 51.
2 K. Marx, *Critique of the Gotha Program*, in D. McLellan, *Marx*, op. cit., p. 70.

tion. Communists "only interpret social development and aid it in various ways; ... nobody can change it".[1]

Desire and historical necessity, ought and shall, are identical. And so are knowledge and will: I want what I know. I want communism and I know it will happen, as soon as historical conditions are advanced enough to make people know that communism is what they want and is what will happen. Practice, historical practice, is the basis of communist theory, and then the theory is the basis for a new historical practice. To will is to say yes to historical development.

Moreover, the truth and the good are equal. The result of historical development is both good and true. The workers who try to realize the movement of history are also working for a better world free from oppression and egoism.

Russia and China

Communism also uses the metaphor of the verdict. "History is the judge — its executioner, the proletarian".[2] The proletariat merely executes the verdict that history has passed on capitalism and that nobody can change. It can execute this verdict because communism has taught it how to do it and because it has an effective political program and effective action plans.

Communism combines the requirement of being at a certain stage of historical development with the necessity of political action. However, the historical attempts to create a communist society have neglected this and have given priority to political action. Russia and China (but also Cuba, Cambodia, etc.) were countries which lacked the historical and material prerequisites for a communist revolution yet still experienced one. The revolutions in these countries were

---

1 K. Popper, *The Poverty of Historicism*, op. cit., p. 52.

2 K. Marx, *Speech at the Anniversary of the People's Paper*, in R.C. Tucker, op. cit., p. 578.

mainly the product of ideas, agitation and organization, not of capitalism overdeveloping. Communist leaders in these countries acted against the core of communism, against historical materialism which states that a communist revolution can occur only in the most advanced capitalist and industrialized countries, so certainly not in Russia in 1917 or in China after World War II. The revolutions there were not supported by an extremely oppressed industrial proletariat united by the modern forces of production. Oppressed farmers, organized and indoctrinated by professional communists, were the driving forces.

The success of these revolutions (success at least in the sense that they occurred at all) shows that the leaders focused more on political actions, indoctrination, agitation and the appeal of a better future than on historical development and material prerequisites. And they had to modify communist theory because of this.

Capitalism can only be overthrown where it exists. Or better, where it is developed to the extreme. The Russian and Chinese revolutions were therefore not orthodox communist revolutions. As François Furet has stated,[1] they were more like coups d'état by small, well-organized groups of revolutionaries, made possible by the circumstances (a world war in both cases, combined with oppressive feudal rule).

Most communist movements, including the few which still exist today (Cuba, Nepal, Peru, etc.), decide the tension in communism between, on the one hand, material determination and fatalism and, on the other, activism and idealism, in favor of the latter. Orthodox communism also attributes an important role for activism and consciousness, but only in the correct material circumstances. Historical necessity creates

---

1 F. Furet, *Le passé d'une illusion*, Lafont, Paris, 1995.

consciousness and action, which will then fasten this necessity. Most communist activists forget this.

Legality

Communism is revolutionary. It doesn't want to work in the system in order to improve it. It wants a radically new system. It doesn't believe in legality, in the use of legal means to reform an existing situation, in the democratic struggle for a workers' government, in proletarian laws, etc. Legality is insufficient to produces the required changes. A complete revolutionary overthrow of the existing system is required. The state structures should not be used but destroyed. Property should not be redistributed but abolished. It's not suffrage or representation that gives power, but ownership. And the legal and political means to enforce the relations of ownership are but secondary tools of power.

Since the owners of the means of production will not accept expropriation peacefully, not even when it is decided by a law and a democratic majority, a violent revolution and a dictatorship of the proletariat is necessary. Reform is unable to produce communism. Communism requires not the modification of society through reform, but the replacement of society with a new one.

> "For us the issue cannot be the alteration of private property but only its annihilation, not the smoothing over of class antagonisms but the abolition of classes, not the improvement of existing society but the foundation of a new one".[1]

The class struggle cannot be solved within the existing system. It results from private ownership. Not from some kind of unjust distribution of private ownership but from its

---

1 Marx, Engels, *Address of the Central Committee to the Communist League*, in R.C. Tucker, op. cit., p. 505.

existence *tout court*. Only in a new system, without owner-ship, can it be solved.

Of course, there are many kinds of communism, and even in the writings of Marx and Engels we can sometimes find some kind of vindication of legality, for example when they speak of the "legislative recognition of particular interests of the workers".[1]

> "The Communist Manifesto had already proclaimed the winning of universal suffrage, of democracy, as one of the first and most important tasks of the militant proletariat".[2] "Every pacific concession of the [ruling classes] ... the English working class know not how to wield their power and use their liberties, both of which they possess legally".[3] "[T]he intelligent use which the German workers made of the universal suffrage intro-duced in 1866".[4] "And if universal suffrage had offered no other advantage than that it allowed us to count our numbers every three years; that by the regularly established, unexpectedly rapid rise in the number of our votes it increased in equal measure the workers' certainty of victory and the dismay of their opponents, and so became our best means of propaganda; that it accurately informed us concerning our own strength and that of all hostile parties, and thereby provided us with a measure of proportion for our actions second to none, safeguarding us from untimely timidity as much as from untimely foolhardiness — if this had been the only advantage we gained from the suffrage, it would still have been much more than enough. But it did more than this by far. In election agitation it provided us with a means, second to none, of getting in touch with the mass of the people where they still stand aloof from us; of forcing all parties to defend their views and actions against our attacks before all the people; and, further, it provided our representatives in the Reichstag with a platform from which they could speak to their oppo-nents in parliament, and to the masses without, with

---

1 Marx, Engels, *The Communist Manifesto*, op. cit., p. 90.

2 F. Engels, *Introduction to The Class Struggles in France*, in R.C. Tucker, op. cit., p. 565.

3 K. Marx, in D. McLellan, *Marx*, op. cit., p. 64.

4 F. Engels, *Introduction to The Class Struggles in France*, in R.C. Tucker, op. cit., p. 565.

quite other authority and freedom than in the press or at meetings".[1] "It is a fact ... that without renouncing his basic revolutionism and the related belief that the socialist revolution would in most countries have to take place by force, Marx envisaged the possibility of a non-violent path to socialism in certain countries, like America and Britain, whose political institutions made radical change by democratic means conceivable ... Lenin contended that conditions in those countries had so changed in the interim that a Marxist could no longer recognize such potential exceptionalism".[2]

But as stated before, even in its original version, communism views legality as the exception, and revolution and violence as the rule.

"We must make clear to the governments : we know that you are the armed power that is directed against the proletariat; we will proceed against you by peaceful means where that is possible and with arms when it is necessary".[3]

"Above all things, the workers must counteract, as much as is at all possible, during the conflict and immediately after the struggle, the bourgeois endeavors to allay the storm, and must compel the democrats to carry out their present terrorist phrases. Their actions must be so aimed as to prevent the direct revolutionary excitement from being suppressed again immediately after the victory. On the contrary, they must keep it alive as long as possible. Far from opposing so-called excesses, instances of popular revenge against hated individuals or public buildings that are associated only with hateful recollections, such instances must not only be tolerated but the leadership of them taken in hand".[4]

Proletarian violence is always counter-violence, self-defense, revolutionary violence used against the violent rule of

---

1 Ibid., p. 566.

2 R.C. Tucker, op. cit., p. xxxvi.

3 K. Marx, *To a conference of the International*, in D. McLellan, *Marx*, op. cit., p. 64-65.

4 Marx, Engels, *Address of the Central Committee to the Communist League*, in R.C. Tucker, op. cit., p. 506-507.

the bourgeoisie, and dictatorial violence used against the rebellious reactionaries. If legality is used and recommended by communism, then as a means to abolish it.

> "With this successful utilization of universal suffrage, however, an entirely new method of proletarian struggle came into operation, and this method quickly developed further. It was found that the state institutions, in which the rule of the bourgeoisie is organized, offer the working class still further opportunities to fight these very state institutions".[1] "To keep this growth going [the growth of the German Social Democratic Party] without interruption until it of itself gets beyond the control of the prevailing governmental system, not to fritter away this daily increasing shock force in vanguard skirmishes, but to keep it intact until the decisive day, that is our main task".[2] "Democracy is of great importance for the working class in its struggle for freedom against the capitalists. But democracy is by no means a limit one may not overstep; it is only one of the stages in the course of development from feudalism to capitalism, and from capitalism to communism".[3]

Order Without a State

In communism, there will be no more economic or political oppression because the equal ownership of the means of production has abolished all classes and hence also the need for a state apparatus for the protection of class relations. However, there will be no more oppression of *classes*. Individual criminal actions will continue to be suppressed, even in communism, but this can happen without a state.

> "This will be done by the armed people itself, as simply and as readily as any crowd of civilized people ... parts a pair of combatants or does not allow a woman to be outraged".[4]

1 F. Engels, *Introduction to The Class Struggles in France*, in R.C. Tucker, op. cit., p. 566.

2 Ibid., p. 571.

3 V.I. Lenin, *Selected Works vol. 7*, p. 91.

4 V.I. Lenin, *State and Revolution*, in *Heritage of Western Civilization*, Prentice Hall, New Jersey, 1987, p. 291.

Moreover, many of these individual actions will disappear in communism because they result from a certain form of society and from oppression. People's behavior can be modified by modifying the economic circumstances.

> "From the moment when private ownership of movable property developed, all societies in which this private ownership existed had to have this moral injunction in common : Thou shalt not steal. Does this injunction thereby become an eternal moral injunction? By no means. In a society in which all motives for stealing have been done away with, in which therefore at the very most only lunatics would ever steal, how the preacher of morals would be laughed at who tried solemnly to proclaim the eternal truth : Thou shalt not steal!".[1] "[F]reed from ... the infamies of capitalist exploitation, people will gradually become accustomed to observing the elementary rules of social life ... without the special apparatus for compulsion which is called the state".[2]

International Communism

Of course, the proletarian state will disappear, not when the last capitalist citizen has given up, but when there are no more other capitalist states that threaten it. Communism has to be global, because capitalist exploitation is global. And because capitalists abroad will react when their fellow capitalists are expropriated.

> "Marx criticized the leaders of the French proletariat in 1848 for thinking that they would be able to consummate a proletarian revolution within the national walls of France, side by side with the remaining bourgeois nations".[3] "On the Continent the revolution is imminent and will immediately assume a socialist character. Is it not bound to be crushed in this little corner,

---

1 F. Engels, *Anti-Dühring*, in R.C. Tucker, op. cit., p. 726.

2 V.I. Lenin, *Selected Works vol. 7*, op. cit. p. 81.

3 D. McLellan, *Marx*, op. cit., p. 65.

considering that in a far greater territory the movement of bourgeois society is still in the ascendant?"[1]

The answer is "yes", of course. And that is why communism must crawl out of its corner, and must become imperialist and expansionist.

1 K. Marx, *Letter to Engels (1858)*, in R.C. Tucker, op. cit., p. 676.

Chapter 5. Evaluation

Control Over Production, Property

This concludes my short but, I hope, honest and objective description of communism. Now, what can we learn from it? I realize that, for many people, learning from communism is like listening to the devil. But that's intellectual laziness, dismissing something without fully understanding it. So bear with me.

For example, our capitalist systems have shed many of the extreme injustices that characterized them in the time of Marx. But it's still the case today that ownership of the means of production yields a kind of economic power over the workers who depend on the owners and who are forced to sell their labor power because they don't have means of production of their own.

This dependence results in economic uncertainty and possibly poverty, because of the competition between workers trying to offer the best deal to employers. The fact that no modern economy has full employment makes this competition inevitable, even though today it's more an international than a national competition. The "reserve army" now seems to be stationed abroad. International outsourcing (or the threat of it) pushes wages down.[1]

We should also acknowledge that economic dependence in a system of private ownership of the means of production can be psychologically detrimental in the sense that it makes creative productive activity, self-expression and self-development (which require the free use of means of production) very difficult if not impossible. Moreover, it means that people are forced to work in systems based on discipline, supervision and control. Corporations have become islands of authoritarianism in a democratic world. If democracy and self-government are important in politics, why not in business?

Given the importance of work and production in the life of an individual and their potentially beneficial role in personal self-development, and given the importance of democracy and self-government, it is justified to give people a say in the way in which the means of production are used. The owners of the means of production should not be entitled to decide unilaterally on the conditions, organization, purposes, processes and meaning of production. Production is an important part of human life and people should have a say in it.

Concretely, this means a kind of corporate democracy and corporate participation. Participation, not by the shareholders (corporate democracy is today mostly viewed as a right of shareholders), but by the people directly involved in production, i.e., the "workers".

Communism traditionally proposes the end of the employment relationship (or the right to rent people) and the

---

1 Geishecker/Goerg, International outsourcing and wages: winners and losers, http://www.etsg.org/ETSG2004/Papers/Geishecker.pdf

common ownership of the means of production as the ways to achieve this participation and to abolish so-called alienation (which means working for a wage, or working in an obscure system of division of labor, rather than working for a product). The workers in the factory, rather than the capitalists or the shareholders, would own the factory and all the assets in common. Or, more correctly, society as a whole, which in communism means the class of workers, would own the totality of all means of production, because otherwise the workers would be tied to one specific means of production and wouldn't be able to switch freely to another one.

This would obviously spell the end of private property, not necessarily private property as such, but in any case private property of the means of production.

This is unacceptable because private property is an important value. It's unequal distribution should be criticized, as well as the exclusive right of decision of the owners of the means of production, but there are good reasons to keep the right to private property more or less intact (or, more specifically, the right to legal protection of private property and the right to use it freely). First of all, private property is a means to protect the private space and privacy. Without private property, without your own house or your own place in the world, and without your own intimate and personal things, it is obviously more difficult to have a private life. The four walls of your private house protect you against the public. Without private property, there is no private world.

Secondly, independence, self-reliance, autonomy, and therefore, also freedom, are important values, and these values rely heavily on private property. Private property is also important for the creation and maintenance of relationships. You have your own house and your own place in the world, but not in the world in general. You live in a particular world, in a very concrete social context of friends, family, enemies, neighbors and other types of relationships. A place in the world is always a place in a particular community, even if you have to transcend this community now and again to avoid narrow-mindedness and chauvinism.

Furthermore, property is an important tool in the creative design of your personality, especially, but not exclusively, when you are an artist or a person engaged in some kind of creative production. It is precisely one of the main concerns of communism that creative production is made very difficult by capitalism.

Private property is also a force behind economic growth and development. When people are allowed to keep the fruits of their labor they are more active economically. And it is obvious that without private property there can be no help or generosity. Generosity and the absence of egoism are important for the preservation of a community. And, finally, the right to private property, and in particular, the right to your own house, is linked to the freedom to choose a residence, which again is linked to the freedom of movement, also important values often crushed by communist regimes.

Now, it's true that private property in these examples isn't necessarily private ownership of the means of production. Thus these examples are no argument against the socialization of the means of production as proposed by communism. But private ownership of the means of production protects other types of private ownership (a so-called inverted domino effect), and, more importantly, it is economically valuable. Allowing people to pocket the benefits of privately owned means of production leads to increased economic output and hence increased wealth.

This last argument has often been berated. It's true that it can be used to justify laissez-faire free market economics and oppose state intervention in the economy and redistribution, in which case it is often called "trickle-down economics". Trickle-down economics, also called Reaganomics (due to its association with the policies of Reagan and Thatcher) or supply-side economics, is the theory according to which policies destined to alleviate poverty and redistribute wealth are unnecessary and even counterproductive. The rich should be allowed to become even more wealthy, by imposing very low tax rates on high incomes (or a flat tax, for example) rather than using the tax system to redistribute wealth. The result would be that their wealth would "trickle down" towards those who are less well off.

According to this scenario, government policies should favor the wealthy, which often means that government should have as few policies as possible. For example, government should impose as few taxes as possible, and those it imposes should as low as possible. This will result in an increase in wealth for the rich, which will in turn result in flows of wealth down to those with lower incomes. That's because the rich, when they are allowed to be rich, are more likely to spend their additional income, either through consumption or investment. This spending creates more economic activity and economic opportunities, which in turn generates jobs and hence more income for the less well off.

All boats rise with a rising tide. Redistribution is counterproductive because it will take away the incentives to do well, and hence also take away the possibility of wealth creation and subsequent automatic wealth distribution through "trickling down". All this is reminiscent of laissez-faire and the invisible hand theory.

This doctrine, however, has been refuted. The biggest country in which it has been implemented, the U.S. (with very low tax rates for the rich, compared to other industrialized countries), has seen enormous increases in income inequality. Obviously not all boats have risen on the same tide. Nevertheless, the other extreme — abolishing private property and hence discouraging all wealth creation — doesn't do any good either. I think it's fair to say that one of the major advantages of private property is the boost it gives to wealth creation. And some of this wealth is automatically redistributed in a market economy. Certainly not enough to justify laissez-faire and limit state intervention, but enough to take it seriously.

The only alternative to private ownership of the means of production is their socialization or nationalization. And this implies the organization of society as a whole, society as one big factory, rationally planned. History has shown that this is economically ineffective. It leads to a lack of competition and of individual incentives to do well. It's impossible for a centralized administration to organize a national economy efficiently, to decide what and how much of each product should be produced, where things should go, etc. Socialization and central planning are also politically dictatorial because they leave nothing to individual freedom and quickly extend beyond the field of the economy.

Therefore, the abolition of private property in general or the socialization of the means of production (i.e., turning them into state property) are not how we should go about in our effort to create corporate democracy.

Of course, like most human rights, the right to private property is an important but not an absolute value. It is a limited right which has to be balanced against other rights. There can and should be government organized redistribution of private property from the rich to the poor, especially when market driven redistribution isn't enough to protect the poor from the consequences of insufficient private property (or, in other words, to protect the economic rights of the poor).

However, redistribution, taxation, expropriation, etc. should be used carefully, in view of the numerous important functions of private property. Moreover, since the abolition of private property means concentration of property in the hands of the state, it implies an increase in state power. The more property a state acquires, the weaker the citizen becomes. Weaker not only compared to the state, but also compared to fellow citizens. His fellow citizens will find themselves in a position whereby they can control and intervene in his weakened private space. These risks were clearly observable in the practices of communist states.

Another point about property: you also own your own body. Your body is part of your private property. It is something that is yours; it is the thing *par excellence* that is your own. It is not common to several people and it cannot be given away. It cannot even be shared or communicated. It is the most private thing there is. Owning your body means that you are the master of it. Other people have no say in the use of your body; they should not use it, hurt it or force you to use it in a certain way. This underpins the security rights such as the right to life, the right to bodily integrity, and the prohibition of torture and slavery. It also implies the right to self-determination, and therefore, the right to die. You carry prime responsibility over your own body and life.

Although communism is concerned about capitalist abuses and expropriation of the workers, of their products, their labor power and their bodies, historical communist regimes have not only shown equal appetite for expropriation (they were rightly called "state capitalist systems"), but also cruel disregard for the bodily aspect of property. It is tempting to believe that the inclination of communist regimes to use forced labor and slavery was, at least partially, determined by their disregard of private property, and that this disregard was conditioned by the theory of the socialization of the means of production.

The property of your body can justify private property of material goods. The power of your body and your labor is incorporated in the goods you produce. By working on an object, you mix your labor with the object. If someone wants to take this object away from you and therefore violate your right to private property, he also takes away your labor, which means that he takes away the power of your body. He therefore uses your body, which is incompatible with your right to possess your own body (see John Locke for a more elaborate although not fully successful version of this argument[1]). If man owns his body, he also owns the power of his body and the objects in which this power is incorporated, to the extent that he has not stolen these objects beforehand. This can also be used as an argument in favor of corporate democracy and redistribution. Workers incorporate their labor in the objects they produce, but don't legally own these objects, and their labor power is not fully compensated by wages. And if they should own the products they produce — at least partially because they invest their labor power in products that they initially do not own — it would be strange to claim that they should not have a say in the organization of production.

The right not to be a slave is the negative version of the right to possess your own body. Those who commit slavery (but also those who steal) act as if the bodies of other people are their property, a property that can be bought and sold. Considering other people as your property diminishes the value and dignity of these other people. Other people should not be considered as a means. This justifies corporate democracy because without it, workers or employees are just tools in a production process over which they have no say. We're

1 J. Locke, *Second Treatise of Government*, Hackett, Indianapolis, 1980.

dealing here with an entirely different problem than the one about exploitation.

Common ownership of the means of production, as proposed by traditional communists, is not the only means to create corporate participation and worker control over production. Communism should simply mean the community of workers in a factory or corporation deciding more or less democratically on their work. Modern-day capitalism has in some cases reconciled private ownership with large measures of worker participation. Many decisions in companies are now taken by the owners and the workers together. (This participation is not incompatible with the free market either. A free market is a system between economic agents, not within them). But we should try to go further and extend and deepen this participation in order to make production and work more meaningful.

Private property of the means of production should not be understood as an absolute right to govern the workplace dictatorially. And the abolition of private property is not a prerequisite for corporate democracy. This is evident if we take a look at historical cases of communist rule, where private property was abolished (to some extent) but corporate governance continued much along the same lines as in capitalism. The bosses changed — autocratic party members and government bureaucracy instead of capitalists- but the workers didn't have more influence.

This proves that corporate democracy requires something more or different than common ownership. Private ownership, strictly speaking, gives the employer only the right to label someone a trespasser. [1] So abolishing ownership will not, of itself, change how production takes place. Changes have to

---

1 David Ellerman, *Marxism as a Capitalist Tool*, http://ssrn.com/abstract=1342814.

occur, not on the level of the ownership of the means of production, but on the level of the organization of production.

Power, Democracy and Human Rights

The private ownership of the means of production, that characterizes most if not all of today's economies, has been economically very successful, against the predictions of communism. It does produce crises now and again, but always seems to recover. We're still waiting for its cataclysmic end.

But I think we should admit that communism was right to claim that it produces alienation and yields an unfair share of economic power, and that this has to be corrected by way of some kind of worker participation in the corporation. We should also admit that this private ownership gives the owners an unfair share of political power, even in a democracy. This is especially the case when the means of production also and increasingly includes the means of information production (news, TV, movies, etc.).

From the point of view of the defenders of democracy, that's a highly relevant criticism, and its relevance hasn't decreased during the century and a half since it was first expressed. On the contrary. It is relatively uncontroversial to say that in all democracies the owners of the means of production influence democratic processes with financial means (lobbying, campaign financing or outright corruption), with ideological means — as was already known to Marx — but also with information technology. They use the means of information production in such a way that they continue to own these and other means of production. Disparities in economic power tend to distort the democratic process because this process is based on the ideal of equal influence and the equal importance of everyone's interests.

But that's an ideal. Existing democracy, as opposed to ideal democracy, often pays more attention to the interests of the wealthy classes rather than the interests of the people in general, in which case it is perverted. The purely formal abolition of the difference between rich and poor in a democracy — every citizen has one vote and as many rights as the next citizen — cannot hide the reality that some citizens can influence policies and public opinion much more than others and hence have more power. The difference is only abolished formally; in reality, democracy may serve to widen it on account of the fact that relatively powerful individuals or groups can use democracy and rights to become even more powerful and influential.

The communist theory that politics is a capitalist tool or that the state is a capitalist machine, has had an enormous success, even with people who are not communists or even anti-communists. Who is not convinced that, for example, the numerous military or covert interventions of the United States elsewhere in the world serve the interests of American companies and American economic supremacy in general? Or that the elections in democracies are heavily biased by big business which wants politics to serve certain interests and tries to get this done by funding candidates, lobbying officials, indoctrinating the public through the ownership of the media, etc.

The reason for this success is that the theory is based on reality. Politics is to some degree influenced by the economy and communism is still relevant to us today because it reminds us of this and because it was the first theory to systematically expose this. Also relevant and significant today is the theory that oppression is not only a power thing but is also based on ideology, information, covert persuasion and even mind control.

What we have to reject is the communist insistence on determination. Politics and narratives are influenced but not completely determined by economics. According to communism, the superstructure of consciousness, religion, morality, politics and law is a mere product of the substructure of productive forces and class relations. Even if politics, for example, influences the economy, it does so only after it was first determined by the economy.

Contrary to this, we must accept that politics can be much more than violent oppression, ideological indoctrination or perversion of democracy for the purpose of maintaining class and property relations. In a democracy especially, we see that politics can be a powerful tool for people to determine and control their common destinies and to expose and undo economic injustices.

Redistribution of wealth from the rich to the poor is possible in a democracy. The poor can use their rights to makes their case and can elect their own representatives in order to enact policies that are favorable to them. Redistribution not only makes life for the poor a bit less painful, but also grants them more political influence and renders democracy a bit less "formal". Other measures enhance the independence of political parties with regard to wealthy pressure groups (for example public instead of private funding for political parties, subsidies for independent TV channels, etc.).

> "What is necessary is that political parties be autonomous with respect to private demands, that is, demands not expressed in the public forum and argued for openly by reference to a conception of the public good. If society does not bear the costs of organization, and party funds need to be solicited from the more advantaged social and economic interests, the pleadings of these groups are bound to receive excessive attention".[1]

1 J. Rawls, *A Theory of Justice*, Oxford University Press, Oxford, 1999, p. 198.

The financing of political parties in a democracy is a controversial matter, especially in a democracy such as the US where parties and candidates have to spend huge amounts of money on advertising and promotion in highly mediatized campaigns. If parties and candidates have to rely on private donations, there is indeed the danger of unequal influence: parties are likely to listen more closely to the requests and opinions of private groups, and these groups then acquire more influence than the ordinary citizen. A democracy should try to achieve the ideal of equal influence.

Few people believe that democracy is a simple and mechanical translation of money flows. Politics, like consciousness and thinking, is obviously much more than ideological shadows of the light of economic reality. Just as religion is much more than opium for the people. It has many beneficial effects which we need not mention here (and I say this as an agnostic). Even if it is a bag of illusions, which no one and not even Marx can prove, it is still a fact that religious illusions can have morally beneficial effects and can make life easier to bear. So why try to strip people of their illusions — which has proven very difficult anyway — for the sake of a better yet uncertain future?

It is wrong to claim, as communism often does, that the economic perversion of democracy is a necessity. Communism sometimes acknowledges that improvements in the situation of the workers — better wages, better labor conditions, unemployment benefits — can be the product of rights claims and of participation in democratic politics.

> "The irony of world history turns everything upside down. We, the 'revolutionists', the 'overthrowers' we are thriving far better on legal methods than on illegal methods and overthrow. The parties of Order, as they call themselves, are perishing under the legal conditions created by themselves. They cry despairingly with Odilon Barrot : la légalité nous tue, legality is the

> death of us; whereas we, under this legality, get firm muscles and rosy cheeks and look like life eternal".[1]

> "After a thirty years' struggle ... the English working classes ... succeeded in carrying the Ten Hours' Bill. The immense physical, moral and intellectual benefits hence accruing to the factory operatives ... are now acknowledged on all sides. Most of the Continental governments had to accept the English Factory Act in more or less modified forms, and the English Parliament itself is every year compelled to enlarge its sphere of action".[2]

However, these are mere footnotes in communist theory. In most cases, communism demands revolution and an entire change of system, based no longer on the private ownership of the means of production. Private ownership softened by social-democracy or by economic rights, by legally enforced improvements for the workers, is not enough. It doesn't have to be softened but replaced by the community of the means of production, or communism. Communist lip service to legality, scarce as it is, is probably only a strategic effort to convert as many movements as possible to the cause of communism:

> "It was very difficult to frame the thing so that our view should appear in a form acceptable from the present standpoint of the workers' movement ... It will take time before the reawakened movement allows the old boldness of speech".[3]

Not all human problems are caused by the private ownership of the means of production, and many can be solved by other means than socialization. Communism fails to acknowledge the importance of legality, and particularly of democratic participation in legislation and of the use of human rights (especially economic rights) to improve the the situ-

---

1 F. Engels, *Introduction to The Class Struggles in France*, in R.C. Tucker, op. cit., p. 571-572.

2 K. Marx, *Inaugural Address of the Working Men's International Association*, in R.C. Tucker, op. cit., p. 517.

3 K. Marx, in R.C. Tucker, op. cit., p. 512.

ation of those who are worst of. Human rights are more than the right to private property. They include economic rights and the participation in democracy by workers' representatives. The effective exercise of these rights, rather than the revolutionary creation of a new society, can lead to some level of redistribution of property (and hence less poverty), better working conditions, corporate participation (and hence the mitigation of economic dependence and the lack of economic power of those who do not own the means of production), and some rebalancing of the disproportionate political power of the wealthy.

No matter how strong the influence, the economy and economic power do not completely determine politics and law. Human rights and democratic participation can and do change the economy. Human rights are more than purely formal, and certainly more than false consciousness, convincing the people that they are equal when they are not, and thereby deflating any pressure for change and maintaining the status quo. They can give power to those who want to change the economy. This is insufficiently acknowledged by communism. It is even likely that communism's rejection of rights and democracy as bourgeois exploitation tools has facilitated human rights violations of totalitarian communist regimes.

Sometimes, Marx and Engels acknowledge that law is not the simple translation of power relations.

> "As soon as the new division of labor which creates professional lawyers becomes necessary, another new and independent sphere is opened up which, for all its general dependence on production and trade, still has also a special capacity for reacting upon these spheres. In a modern state, law must not only correspond to the general economic condition and be its expression, but must also be an internally coherent expression which does not, owing to inner contradictions, reduce itself to nought. And in order to achieve this, the faithful reflection of economic conditions suffers increasingly.

> All the more so the more rarely it happens that a code
> of law is a blunt, unmitigated, unadulterated expres-
> sion of the domination of a class — this in itself would
> offend the 'conception of right'. Even in the Code Na-
> poléon the pure, consistent conception of right held
> by the revolutionary bourgeoisie of 1792–96 is already
> adulterated in many ways, and, in so far as it is embod-
> ied there, has daily to undergo all sorts of attenuations
> owing to the rising power of the proletariat".[1]

Law is here determined both by the economy and by the
principle of coherence. However, this concession is too limited. Law can also be influenced by other elements, for example
morality. If we revisit figure 2, we should admit that arrow
2 can come from elsewhere as well, and that arrow 3 is not
necessarily a force for the status quo but can also change the
relations of production.

Real and Formal Equality

According to communism, democracy suffers from a contradiction between formal political and judicial equality on
the one hand (equal votes but also equal rights, equality before the law, etc.) and real economic or material inequality on
the other hand. The latter prevents the full realization of the
former. Wealthy persons have more means (such as money,
time, and education) to inform themselves, to lobby, to influence, to get themselves elected, to defend themselves in court,
etc. A merely formal principle such as political or judicial
equality loses much of its effectiveness when some can use
their wealth to control or at least influence political and judicial debates and decisions.

Communism claims that the equality of political rights
(democracy) and human rights (not only the right to private
property) serves to cover up, justify and maintain material
inequality, exploitation and class rule in a capitalist society.

1 F. Engels, *Letter to J. Bloch (1890)*, in R.C. Tucker, op. cit., p. 762-763.

Real material equality and therefore also real political, judicial and legal equality can only be brought about by an anticapitalist revolution which brings down the capitalist system of property along with the legal, judicial and democratic political tools that are used to protect this property.

Material redistribution through taxation, unemployment benefits, healthcare systems and so forth is not enough because it does not affect material inequality in a substantial way. It only provides a minimum of basic goods, not a radically egalitarian distribution. The remaining material inequality, and more specifically the inequality of the ownership of the means of production, still engenders unequal economic, political and judicial power. Democracy is self-defeating. It can never deliver what it promises because it does not go far enough. It can only give people formal instead of substantial equality. Elections, rotation in office, economic rights, and equality before the law are superficial phenomena without effect on the deeper economic processes of exploitation and class rule. Democracy must therefore be replaced by something better.

Communism claims that there can only be real political equality and real equality of power when the most important goods — the means of production — are the equal property of all citizens. In all other cases, the rich will have more opportunities to benefit from political participation and judicial protection. Equal rights will lead to an unequal outcome, and this is of course the purpose of the system.

Much of this is, of course, correct, as stated above. Wealthy groups can and do use elections, the judicial system and human rights to pursue their interests, often at the expense of less fortunate groups. They may even use democracy to maintain exploitation. They can speak better thanks to their education; they have a better knowledge of the ways in which to defend interests; they know their rights; they have friends in high places, they have resources to lobby or bribe; they control the means of communication and information.

But rather than destroying the private ownership of the means of production, compensating measures can be taken, not only in order to respect economic rights and redistribute goods and opportunities so that everyone has the necessary minimum of these, but also in order to respect political rights

It is clear that we are not dealing with a potentially fatal argument against democracy and human rights. Wealth causes political inequality everywhere, not just in a democracy. Democracy and human rights are in fact the only solution to the problem of the unequal political result of economic inequality because they can provide compensating measures. They may not be able to neutralize the influence of wealth entirely, but that's possibly not even a desirable goal, as is shown by the history of radically egalitarian regimes that have taken this goal seriously.

Democracy and human rights are not merely formal. Equal voting power, equality before the law and equal rights do not cover up and do not maintain the social division between rich and poor. Democracy does not hide divisions; it shows them and it shows them in a better way than any other form of government. And because it allows divisions to become public, it offers the best chance of eliminating or softening unjust divisions. Democracy does not only serve the interests of the wealthy classes. Poor, exploited or oppressed groups also benefit from freedom of expression, from the election of their own representatives and from the possibility to claim rights (economic rights, for instance, which also equalize political influence because they create leisure time and time for politics). Even the bare fact of being able to show an injustice is an advantage in the struggle against this injustice. If you are not able to see an injustice — and this can happen in an unfree society — then you are not aware of its existence and you can do nothing about it. Democracy at least gives poverty a voice, and, as they say, the squeaky hinge gets the oil.

The struggle against injustice means questioning society and the powers that be (also the economic powers). It is easier to question social relationships in a society in which political power can be questioned. Publicly questioning political power in a democracy is a process in which the entire people, rich and poor, are involved. This process legitimizes the act of questioning per se and therefore also the act of questioning injustices in society.[1] Elections and rights are not a force against change. They create infinite possibilities, including the possibility to change economic structures.

Of course, the political and legal elimination of the difference between rich and poor (they all have an equal vote, equal rights and equality before the law) does not automatically result in the elimination of the social difference between rich and poor, nor does it necessarily result in equal political and legal power or influence. However, democracy and human rights can diminish the influence of property and wealth because they give legal and political means to the poor in order to defend their interests; no other form of government performs better in this field because no other form of government gives the same opportunities to the poor (the opportunity to show injustices, to elect representatives, to lobby governments, to claim rights and so on).

If certain divisions are made politically and legally irrelevant (by way of equal rights, equality before the law, equal vote), then this is not necessarily part of a conscious strategy to maintain these divisions in real life. If it were part of such a strategy, it would probably produce the opposite of what

---

1 Cl. Lefort, *L'invention démocratique*, Fayard, Paris, 1994.

is intended. The chances that injustices disappear are much higher in a society in which injustices can be shown and questioned, and a democracy is the best example of this kind of society. A society which can question itself because it can question the relations of power is more likely to change. This is shown by the recent history of most western democracies where many injustices have been abolished by way of democracy and human rights. The labor movement, the suffragette movement and feminism would have been much more difficult without democracy and rights, which is shown by the reality of workers and women in contemporary societies that enjoy less freedom than western democracies. Western workers, women, immigrants, etc. have all made successful use of the possibility to claim rights, to elect representatives, to enact legislation and thereby reduce inequality.

Political influence will probably never be equal for everybody (talent also plays a role, and it is difficult to correct for the effects of talent). But there is more and there is less. Democracy is probably the best we can hope for. On top of that, democracy constantly enhances the equality of influence, even though every victory creates a new problem. The internet, for example, empowers many people and enhances political equality, but it also excludes many other people, namely those without the necessary computer skills or without the infrastructure necessary to use the internet on an equal basis. It can become a new source of political inequality. We will have to finds ways in which to equalize the access to and the use of the internet because we want to maintain or increase political equality. In the meanwhile, however, a new kind of inequality should not make us lose sight of the enormous progress for equality which the internet allowed us to achieve. Many people, who today use the internet to participate in politics, never participated in the past.

The communist criticism of capitalist and democratic politics can be maintained because it is partially correct. However, rather than rejecting democratic politics, we must strive to improve it. Also, the idea of egalitarianism that is inherent in the concept of a classless society is worth keeping, albeit not in its radical form and not limited to equality of social-economic classes. Equal rights and equal political influence remain unfinished business. The effort to end discrimination against women, immigrants, LGBT (lesbian, gay, bisexual, and transgender people), castes, etc., while not prominent in traditional communist thinking, can be based on the egalitarianism inherent in communism, but on the condition that we understand that not all forms of inequality are based on the economy.

Human Rights and Egoism

Communism views human rights as primarily directed against fellow citizens. It's true that human rights can be used to protect oneself against attacks from other citizens or from the state, but communism sees this protection as an egoistic act by those with economic power who wish to defend themselves against economic claims by the poor. Human rights are seen as egoistic rights aimed at the status quo: they serve to protect an economic position. This is supposed to be evident from the fact that the only thing human rights tell us to do for other people is to avoid doing certain things. Hence their tendency to maintain the status quo. If human rights only require forbearance and no assistance, then how are they supposed to help the poor and destroy the status quo?

According to communism, human rights are the "rights of the egoistic man, separated from his fellow men and from the community".[1] They are the rights of man as an isolated,

---

1 Marx in Tucker, op.cit., p. 43.

inward looking, self-centered creature, who regards his free opinion as his intellectual private property instead of a part of communication; who uses his right to private property not in order to create a beach-head for his public life but to accumulate unnecessary wealth and to protect unequal property relationships; who uses the right to privacy as a wall keeping out the poor snoopers watching the rich people; who considers fellow men as nothing more than the only legitimate restraint on his own freedom, and therefore as a limit instead of the source of his own thinking, identity and humanity (this is the way in which communism reads art. 6 of the French constitution of 1793: "Liberty is the power which man has to do everything which does not harm the rights of others"). Communism views human rights as the rights of a man who considers freedom to be no more than the ability to pursue selfish interests and to enjoy property, unhindered by the need to help other people, "without regard for other men and independently of society"[1]; and who considers equality to be the equal right to this kind of freedom (in theory, everybody can emancipate himself by becoming a bourgeois since the bourgeoisie is an "open" class compared to, for example, the aristocracy).

Human rights, in this view, serve only to protect egoism and the unequal distribution of property, and to oppress the poor who question this and who try to redistribute property. On top of that, human rights obscure this fact because they are formulated in such a way that it seems that everybody profits equally from them. Contrary to what is implicit in their name, "human" rights are not general or universal rights. They are the rights of those who have property and who want to keep it.

---

1 Ibid., p. 42.

However, this is an unwarranted limitation of the meaning of human rights. Human rights are also positive rights in the sense that they impose a duty on citizens to do something. They do not stop at the prohibition of interference. This is most evident in economic rights. When somebody is starving, everybody is obliged to help and to give some of his or her goods to the person in need. This person has a right to such assistance. Forbearance, non-interference and leaving the other person alone will not protect this person's rights.

And when this right to assistance comes into conflict with the right to private property, a correct and just balance should be struck between these two rights. The system of human rights isn't a harmonious whole. Rights aren't always compatible, and sometimes one right has to give way for another.

Other types of rights are also more than just instruments to keep people out of each other's way ("rights as zoo-keepers"). Freedom of expression is used to convince other people, to create groups, to impress other people, etc. Letting people do what they do without interference is therefore not enough to respect another person's right to free speech. You have to listen, and you have to be open to the possibility of being convinced. Free expression and the right to free speech would lose their value in any other case. However, this doesn't mean that the right to free speech implies a duty of others to listen. It only means that without listening, this right is meaningless. And this is the basis of the claim that the right isn't an egocentric or egoistic right, but a right that only makes sense in a community. The same is true for the much despised right to private property. We already have seen how private property is important for our place in the world and in a community.

Communism was able to criticize rights for their supposed inherent egoism because historically the bourgeoisie considered rights as primarily requiring forbearance. This criticism is aimed at a simplistic view of human rights typical of a very specific historical period and social group. This view is in no way the only possible one. Of course, the criticism can be correct. No one will deny that human rights can serve to protect and justify egoism, oppression of the poor and indifference. They can help to shield people behind private interest and to transform society into a collection of loose, self-centered, self-sufficient, withdrawn, independent, sovereign and isolated individuals. Because the rich have more means to use, for example, their freedom of expression, this freedom can be an instrument of the rich to monopolize political propaganda and political power and to use this power to maintain their privileged situation. Economic relationships can be maintained by legal means.

However, in order to judge and possibly reject a phenomenon, one should look at all it functions, not only at the ways in which it can be abused. Human rights are not per se the rights of egoistic man. They can also be the rights of those people who need relationships and public and cultural life. They not only protect man against the attacks and claims of other people, for example the attacks and claims on his property; they also create the possibility of doing something together in a common world and of equalizing material resources. They do not allow you to do something to other people (taking their property, determining their opinions, etc.), but at the same time they invite you to do something with other people. In other words, they are not only negative. They not only limit the way we relate to other people, but also stimulate and protect the way we relate to other people. Not only private man, but also public man is the object of human rights.

Once human rights are instituted — which means written down in law, enforced in a court of law, and exercised in institutions such as parliaments, referenda, groups in civil society, etc. — they cease to be merely individual rights or rights used for protection against the state or against fellow citizens. Therefore, they cannot be reduced to instruments of extreme individualism or egoism.

Human rights can indeed be viewed as mere fences around the private world, but let us not forget that an exclusive attention to the general interest can be equally dangerous. 20th century communist states in particular have shown that sacrificing the interest of the individual for some supposed general interest can cause widespread human damage, perhaps even more damage than exclusive attention to private interest. When you're not afraid to break an egg in order to make an omelet, you are not motivated by egoism but the harm you can do is potentially even bigger than the harm done by an egoist.

It is true that the historical origins of human rights can be traced to the rise of the western bourgeoisie who needed something new to dismantle the feudal structures of the aristocracy and the powers inhibiting the development of capitalism. The fact that human rights originated from a specific historical situation — the western capitalist revolution — does not imply that they cannot be useful in another time or place, or for purposes that differ from the original ones. Furthermore, this story of the genesis of human rights is far from complete. Important events, before and after the rise of capitalism, as well as events taking place in other cultures, contributed substantially to the formulation and tradition of human rights.

Even though communism made the mistake of dismissing human rights because of one possible use or misuse of human rights, this criticism has helped us become aware of the fact that human rights not only regulate the relationships between the state and its citizens but also the relationships be-tween citizens (albeit also other kinds of relationships than those which communism had in mind).

Of course, the awareness of human rights as positive rights necessary to create relationships, should not lead us to neglect their function as boundaries, boundaries between citizens and the state and between citizens. And this function as boundaries can be beneficial, contrary to what communism claims. Notwithstanding the importance of relationships and communication, there are certain boundaries that neither fellow citizens nor the state can transgress.

Human rights create an inviolable and impregnable space in which the individual can be himself, can make his own decisions and can do as he likes, free and unhindered. This space escapes the control of fellow citizens and of the state. It has been called a space of "petty sovereignty" or "non-interference", similar to the larger space of the sovereign nation state. Freedom of thought, the right to bodily integrity and the right to life are particularly important for the creation of this space. Neither the law nor our fellow citizens should determine what we think, what we do with our bodies or when we stop living. Our space for thinking is free from interference, and the same is true of our physical space, the space of our body and our home. Our free space has a mental as well as a bodily character. Both the mind and the body are inviolable.

Human rights limit the actions and the interference of other people and the state. These limits and boundaries protect us against the state and our fellow citizens. But this protection isn't just a capitalist thing. Everyone needs it, and it's not just about protecting property and the status quo.

However, the negative aspect of human rights — the boundary — is not more important than the positive one, the creation of relationships. This duality can be seen in the history of the word "law". The Ancient Greek word for law, "nomos", comes from "nemein," which means to divide or distribute, whereas the Latin word for law, "lex", has a totally different meaning, closer to relationship than separation. "Lex" not only implies coercion or prohibition, but also connection, agreement or contract. If human rights would be no more than borders and protection mechanisms, then politics would be reduced to zoo keeping, keeping the animals apart, and the people would be reduced to "homo homini lupus", wild animals that need to be tamed by the law and by human rights. This is a reductionist vision of politics and society.

Individuality, Thinking

Communism, like romanticism, psychology, anthropology and the experience of colonialism, has thought us that our thinking is contextual and determined to a large extent by our circumstances, our group, our class, our culture, our tradition, etc. Our thinking is not exclusively our own, and neither is it by definition universal and applicable to the rest of the world.

However, man is capable of independent thinking. Not all thinking is determined by our material circumstances, our group, tradition or culture. This seems to be proven by the fact that neither Marx nor Engels were working class. Many people have dedicated their lives to ideals and ideas that were not designed to promote the interests of the class to which they belonged. However, it remains useful to be conscious of the possibility that our thoughts are self-interested reflections of our material position in society.

Communism is one-sided in the sense that it does not seem to understand the ways in which the economy is shaped by economically undetermined (but perhaps differently determined) world-views and values. We already mentioned human rights and democratic participation. Max Weber has studied the influence of Protestantism and Calvinism on the development of capitalism. Certain values, such as the opinion that God will reward those who work hard and save money, or the belief in predestination — getting rich is a sign of God's approval — have had an enormous influence on the economy.

Of course, both the communist bottom-up and the top-down approaches are useful. It cannot be the purpose

> "to substitute for a one-sided materialistic an equally one-sided spiritualistic interpretation of culture and of history. Each is equally possible, but each, if it does not serve as the preparation, but as the conclusion of an investigation, accomplishes equally little in the interest of historical truth".[1]

The influence of the economy on thinking should be accepted, but again there is a difference between influencing and completely determining something. The ancient Greeks or Romans did not develop modern science and the industrial production based on it, partly because their mode of production was based on slavery and did not require industrialization and production improvements based on science.

Another example of an idea determined by the economy: the religious rule of arranged marriages allows the father to choose his successor in the family business. Many ideas and values, scientific and moral, correspond to economic necessities and often this has been forgotten over time. Communism has the merit of making us aware of such things. But not everything is economical in the last analysis. Turning the economy into something absolute means neglecting the importance of intellectual, moral, religious and cultural factors that are more than just products of economic reality.

---

1 Max Weber, *The Protestant Ethic and the Spirit of Capitalism*, Allen & Unwin, London, 1976, p. 183.

Communism sometimes accepts this because it sees the importance of non-economic elements in history. But the main idea is still economic determinism because non-economic elements can only do their work once they themselves have been determined by the economy.

> "According to the materialist conception of history, the ultimately determining element in history is the production and reproduction of real life. More than this neither Marx nor I have ever asserted. Hence if somebody twists this into saying that the economic element is the only determining one, he transforms that proposition into a meaningless, abstract, senseless phrase. The economic situation is the basis, but the various elements of the superstructure: political forms of the class struggle and its results, to wit: constitutions established by the victorious class after a successful battle, etc., juridical forms, and then even the reflexes of all these actual struggles in the brains of the participants, political, juristic, philosophical theories, religious views and their further development into systems of dogmas, also exercise their influence upon the course of the historical struggles and in many cases preponderate in determining their form. There is an interaction of all these elements in which ... the economic movement finally asserts itself as necessary ... We make our history ourselves, but, in the first place, under very definite assumptions and conditions. Among these, the economic ones are ultimately decisive. But the political ones, etc., and indeed even the traditions which haunt human minds also play a part, although not the decisive one".[1]

> "[T]he fatuous notion of the ideologists that because we deny an independent historical development to the various ideological spheres which play a part in history we also deny them any effect upon history. The basis of this is the common undialectical conception of cause and effect as rigidly opposite poles, the total disregarding of interaction. These gentlemen often almost deliberately forget that once a historic element has been brought into the world by other, ultimately economic

1 F. Engels, *Letter to J. Bloch* (1890), in R.C. Tucker, op. cit., p. 760-761.

causes, it reacts, can react on its environment and even on the causes that have given rise to it".[1]

"[T]he whole vast process goes on in the form of inter-action — though of very unequal forces, the economic movement being by far the strongest, most primeval, most decisive".[2]

Contrary to this, we have to accept that non-economical causes count even without first having been influenced by the economy.

History, Science, Utopianism

Communism, the theory of being, of what is, rather than the theory of consciousness and of what we think, is in fact the theory "par exellence" of what *will* be. The future and how we will get there is what communism is really interested in, although it claims that this future and the road toward it are merely conclusions of the analysis of the current and past state of affairs.

This is the basis of the claim that communism is a sci-ence. Communist society is a historical necessity, the result of laws of historical development similar to the laws of na-ture. "[W]e simply have to submit to the existing laws of de-velopment, just as we have to submit to the law of gravity".[3]

Communist society can be but does not have to be some-thing one wants to have, a desire in the light of which one goes to look for evidence that shows that it may happen. It's supposed to be the other way around: one simply looks at the evidence, dispassionately, and then decides that something will happen given this evidence. It is only by chance that our desires about what should happen tend to be confirmed by the facts.

1 F. Engels, *Letter to F. Mehring (1893)*, in R.C. Tucker, op. cit., p. 767.

2 F. Engels, *Letter to J. Bloch (1890)*, in R.C. Tucker, op. cit., p. 765.

3 K. Popper, *The Poverty of Historicism*, op. cit., p. 53.

However, it's not impossible to question these scientific pretensions of communism. Which came first, the interpretation of history as something which produced the vision of progress and a better future? Or the hope for a better future which produced a certain interpretation of history? Even without the possibility of looking inside the minds of communists, it is clear that, for many, the desire and the vision of the future were there first, and that the analysis of reality is biased because it favors those elements that seem to substantiate an evolution in the direction of the desired state of affairs. Rather than dispassionate observers of reality, we see that most communists are (or were) passionate believers in an ideal.

The fact that their predictions, after a century and a half, have not come true (yet) seems to support this. Capitalism obviously still survives today, although currently it looks a bit shaken given the global recession. Compared to the fate of communist experiments, it has done pretty well over time. The current economic crisis, like previous ones, will be overcome without much damage to the system. Some of the (proposed) nationalizations (of banks for example) aren't steps on the way to communism, no matter what certain people on the right predict. They are proposed as temporary emergency measures by people who strongly believe in the free market and private ownership.

Of course, it is impossible to say if the failure of communist predictions is due to the communist claim that capitalism has to do well first before communism can have a chance and that the predictions can still come true. It may also be that the theory about the tensions and contradictions in capitalism is simply wrong, that these tensions or contradictions do not have the effect that communism hoped or claimed they would have, or that capitalism has evolved and adapted itself since the time when communist theory was first formulated.

It is clear that we should abandon the view on history as something representing a vast and necessary evolution. History is a not a whole and does not go anywhere. Which does not mean that certain injustices identified by communism should not be eliminated or that certain of the communist views on society should not be implemented. If, in doing so, we create a better world, then we will have succeeded, but there is nothing necessary or inevitable about all this, and it is certainly compatible with views on history different from the one which sees history as a necessary succession of forms of society.

We don't need a new society in order to change a society. Reform from the inside has proven to be very successful. Improvements in people's lives do not require a modification of the entire form of society or the next step in the evolution of society. In other words, it does not require revolution. Revolution is not the only way to create a better world.

Rather than look for a grand revolution at the end of history as the solution to all injustices, we should try to make the lives of the poor better through piecemeal reform. The communist vision of history as a process of progress, unified and evolving as a whole (a "coherence arises in human history"[1]), is untrue. The desire to have a clear purpose in history, a clean process rather than a volatile and uncertain multi-directional chaos, a plan unfolding and a purpose coming closer, is clearly false, and probably dictatorial in its implications. If change is something that encompasses society as a whole, then those who want to encourage change will decide to take over society as a whole and implement central control

---

1 K. Marx, The Poverty of Philosophy, in D. McLellan, The Thought of Karl Marx, op. cit., p. 142.

Wage, Profit, Corporate Social Responsibility

Communism's disdain for profit and its identification of profit and exploitation may be overkill, but it does have a point. The almost exclusive attention to profit and shareholder revenue in most companies, is ethically indefensible. Companies have other responsibilities than the maximization of profit.

Companies, like any other human entity with the power to act and influence people's lives, should respect human rights and should do all that is possible in order to avoid that its activities somehow violate human rights. This is what is called "corporate social responsibility". This concept describes the responsibilities of corporations or companies to the wider social environment in which they operate. A corporation's responsibilities go beyond profit or the interests and needs of shareholders. They are even wider than the interests of its workers, employees and customers, and include care for the natural environment and for the human rights of people who are affected in some way by its activities.

Potentially, corporate social responsibility is of a global nature, because a company can affect the environment of places far away, and the human rights of people in distant countries. Transnational companies especially may have such a global impact, but other kinds of companies as well. For example, an arms producer doesn't have to be a transnational company in order to be complicit in rights violations in different parts of the world.

So, human rights are part of corporate social responsibility. The activities of companies can violate human rights in various ways. Just a few quick examples. Workers and employees can be forced to accept labor conditions which violate the rights described in articles 23 and 24 of the Universal Declaration:

> Article 23: 1. Everyone has the right to work, to free choice of employment, to just and favorable conditions of work and to protection against unemployment. 2. Everyone, without any discrimination, has the right to equal pay for equal work. 3. Everyone who works has the right to just and favorable remuneration ensuring for himself and his family an existence worthy of human dignity, and supplemented, if necessary, by other means of social protection. 4. Everyone has the right to form and to join trade unions for the protection of his interests.

> Article 24: Everyone has the right to rest and leisure, including reasonable limitation of working hours and periodic holidays with pay.

These labor conditions can even amount to slavery, violating article 4:

> No one shall be held in slavery or servitude; slavery and the slave trade shall be prohibited in all their forms.

Or child labor, violating article 26, granting the right to education. These labor conditions should include the labor conditions in the supply chain and in companies that work as subcontractors (including outsourcing).

Another way in which companies can violate human rights is when their products and services are harmful to the health of its customers, violating articles 3 and 25 granting the right to life, standard of living and health. Apart from directly violating human rights, a company can also be complicit in violations committed by others. It can, for example, sell arms and other commodities to authoritarian and dictatorial governments, or governments engaged in an unjust war. Its economic activity in a country can be beneficial to a dictatorial government and can prop up this government (e.g., buying diamonds from a government exploiting its people).

Many companies have already adopted a code of conduct regulating their responsibilities. They have done so voluntarily or forced by public opinion or consumer action. But others haven't. And there are still numerous companies actively engaging in activities which they know contribute to rights violations. So the question has been raised if companies should be forced to respect human rights. Or, in other words, if corporate social responsibility in general and corporate responsibility for human rights in particular, should be made legally enforceable. And, if so, how this should be done.

Of course, many laws, including human rights laws, already apply to companies and can be used to force companies to respect human rights (for example laws on labor standards, safety, non-discrimination etc.). However, perhaps it would be better to say that many such laws apply to individuals within companies rather than to companies themselves. And that's OK because most of the time, if not always, human rights are violated by individuals. Someone, somewhere in a company, decides to sell arms to a warlord, to invest in a dictatorship, or to impose grossly inadequate labor conditions. It's possible to find a person who is legally responsible. (The International Criminal Court, for example, can prosecute individuals acting in their capacities as directors, employees or agents of corporations.)

However, there are two problems with this kind of reasoning. One problem is that enforcement of laws is difficult in the case of transnational companies or other companies with activities abroad. A company may have its headquarters in one country, which, as it happens, is a country with good laws and good enforcement mechanism. But it's activities generate rights violations elsewhere in the world, in countries that cannot do much about it, either because they are afraid to scare away the company, or because the governments there are complicit in the human rights violations. So there's a problem of enforcement.

And the second problem: it may not be so easy to determine exactly which individual(s) within a company are responsible for the harmful activities of the company. A few solutions to these two problems have been proposed. Countries can include extra-territoriality in their national legislation. Companies can then be prosecuted by the country in which they have their headquarters, and under the law of this country, even if the violations have occurred elsewhere. Another proposed solution is more troublesome: make companies separate entities punishable by (international) law, like individuals and states already are. I see some problems with this one. It would allow individual perpetrators to hide behind their companies and escape responsibility. And it would mean, in some case, that people are punished for the misbehavior of their company. For example, if a company is held liable for rights violations, and forced to pay damages which lead to bankruptcy, the company's employees would suffer, even though they carry no responsibility for the actions of the company (or for the actions of those in the company making the decisions). That would be collective punishment, which is a morally odious concept.

All this is still embryonic and the focus of capitalism is still clearly on profit. However, notwithstanding this focus, in the West at least we have not witnessed increased exploitation of workers as a means to increase profit. On the contrary, a certain balance has been achieved between company profit on the one hand and fair wages and good working conditions on the other. Most people get a wage that is higher than the price for the simple reproduction of labor power. And the conditions in which they work are steadily improving. All this is, to a large extent, because of the way in which workers have claimed and used their human rights and their role in democratic politics. Companies have also understood that they need consumers for their goods and services and that exploiting the workers is self-destructive.

However, profit and pressure rather than moral conviction or a sense of responsibility seem to be the main causes of these improvements. One can also argue that the balance was achieved, not because of pressure or the self-interested realization of the destructiveness of exploitation, but on the basis of colonial and neocolonial exploitation. Exploitation was exported. This balance is now being upset by globalization, a phenomenon which can be explained in communist terms. Globalization is in part the search for people who are willing to work for lower wages and longer hours. However, it's too simple to see this as exploitation, since the outsourced jobs offer, in general, much better conditions to the workers in developing countries than the more traditional local jobs.

Another possible explanation of the creation of a balance is technology. History has indeed been characterized by a steadily increasing level of technological control over nature and this has been a kind of liberation. Freedom indeed requires freedom from natural needs and hence requires technology and industry. The continuous development of technology and industry has made life easier for workers, both in the workplace and at home. It has offset the need to increase labor intensity and to decrease wages.

However, liberation does not necessarily mean freedom. The communist conception of freedom, much like the capitalist one, sometimes tends to be rather negative. It is the absence of something, namely the absence of exploitation and of natural necessity. One should also theorize about a positive conception of freedom such as autonomy or self-realization. Liberated from toil and oppression, there is indeed the possibility of something else, but for what? Leisure, consumption, self-development, private or public matters? Communism says it is self-development through free and creative production by people owning their means of production and not having to work for a wage or for a product they don't understand. But it does not say what this requires whereas it is clear that it requires culture, education, rights and real corporate participation, not just state capitalism. But communism is vague about these matters in communist society, or even dismissive. We saw that it fails to adequately conceptualize corporate democracy and that it claims that there is no state in communism. But if there's no state, how will the institutional prerequisites for individual development then be protected? It's naive to believe that the end of property and scarcity will mean the end of the need for personal protection. People will still violate each other's rights, making it difficult to engage in self-development, free creative production, education, and culture.

Moreover, communism is completely oblivious about the negative consequences of control over nature. Ecology has no place in communism. Freedom from natural necessity can mean control over nature in order to better fulfill our needs, or it can also mean control over our needs, which is a much more ecological stance.

Production

There is a balance, in the West at least, between profit and the well-being of workers, but many workers still work for their wages and consider their daily tasks as a toil, not in most cases a physical toil but a psychological one, because they work in systems they don't understand, let alone control, or because they contribute an insignificant, detailed part. Many people go to work, not to produce, be creative or self-develop, but simply to make a living, to have some prestige, money, status, power or other goods external to the creative production process in which they engage or the product to which they contribute.[1] Work is no longer or still not connected with who we are or wish to become. Who does not dream of some other life? The statistics about job satisfaction and job motivation are depressing.[2] The focus of communism on creativity, development, variety and self-expression rather than wages and survival as the goals of labor is very convincing, just as the demand for workers' control of their factories as a means to achieve this. Not entirely convincing is the claim that socialization of the means of production is the only way, or that it is necessary to enhance productivity and to abolish the division of labor.

Further automation since the time of Marx, and especially the computer and the robot, has indeed abolished many monotonous detail tasks previously carried out in a numbing system of division of labor.

> "The proliferation of new, increasingly specialized tasks ... suggest new applications for technology in the production process. Adam Smith points out ... how concentration on a single, simple task frequently suggests new possibilities for machine production that would have escaped the attention of a craftsman dissipating his attention on a variety of tasks; hence the division of labor frequently leads to the creation of new technology, as well as the reverse".[3]

Nevertheless, even if many of us — in the West at least — are no longer machine appendices in the style of Chaplin's "Modern Times", we are still tied to routine jobs that are part

---

1 A. MacIntyre, *After Virtue*, Duckworth, London, 1999, p. 189. The situation outside of the West, in many poor countries, is of course much worse. People there work, not to make a living, but to survive. However, I think it's false to blame capitalism or the free market for this. Many poor developing countries don't have a well-developed capitalist system or a free market. The causes of their poverty can be found elsewhere: bad governance, corruption, the resource curse, poverty traps, the AIDS epidemic etc.

2 See http://www.lifescience.com/health/070226_hate_jobs.html.

3 F. Fukuyama, op. cit., p. 354.

of a system the purpose of which is obscure to us or leaves us indifferent. We feel that our contribution is relatively insignificant and that we are replaceable and we're probably right. It is morally correct to promote polyvalence, variation and individual production and creativity, but not necessarily through socialization and automation. And not with naivety. Many people will never be and will never want to be polyvalent producers.

Division of labor into fragmented tasks in a highly hierarchical organization is probably not so much a requirement of modern production technology but rather the consequence of a very specific way of viewing production relationships (relationships between highly qualified "managers" and simple executors). Other was of viewing production are possible and should be promoted. The division of a production process in elementary parts can indeed increase efficiency and productivity, but this doesn't imply that every task should be assigned exclusively to one person making it his life's calling.

Cooperation and Excellence

An important and valuable aspect of work which has been lost in many activities is cooperation. The modern industrial production process is characterized by unconscious cooperation. The division of labor — within a factory or within the wider economy — is cooperation, but the workers in a factory or the baker and the butcher buying each other's products, are unaware of it. The conscious cooperation of individuals producing something together is more valuable, educating and rewarding for the individuals than individual production or unconscious cooperation which, unfortunately, is the predominant type in capitalist production.

Cooperation also typically transcends the generations. It is important to build on the achievements of the past. So even when you can work alone in a meaningful way, for example as a craftsperson (which perhaps has become rather unlikely these days), you are not really alone because the past masters of the art are looking over your shoulder and guiding you. And maybe you have a pupil.

And here's where another important aspect of work has to be rediscovered in our era of deskilled and atomized production: the standards of excellence.[1] Absorbing the history and tradition of a practice makes us better persons and enables us to produce, be creative, express ourselves and develop our personalities. Without abilities taught to us by tradition this is impossible.

Excellence, as conscious cooperation, is often lacking in contemporary capitalist production. The atomization of workers resulting from the division of labor promotes ever more detailed and limited knowledge, rather than insight in and mastery over processes. Workers are also deskilled because of automation. Skill and knowledge are incorporated into machines and computers, and a worker is still, in many cases, a mere machine-appendix with no need to know how the machine works.

> Communism has rightly accused capitalism of neglecting the need for conscious cooperation and excellence, but it has failed, even theoretically, to offer an alternative. The alternative for unconscious cooperation is real corporate democracy, something that is only hinted at in communist theory and not likely to follow from the simple abolition of private property. Likewise, the communist solution to the problem of excellence — the end of division of labor — isn't satisfactory. Excellence or skill require education institutions and encouraging and supporting communities, which are often lacking or underperforming in industrial societies. The days of the atomized workers in anonymous industrial cities and extremely compartmented factories may be gone (in the West at least), but capital-

---

1 A. MacIntyre, op. cit., p. 187.

> ism still isn't known for its ability to foster supporting communities. And neither is communism. Only with supporting educational institutions and communities, individuals can become someone, learn something and transform themselves through the activity of work.

It is obvious that corporate democracy is not enough to achieve this focus on excellence. And neither is the abolition of the division of labor. On the contrary. Excellence and skill require some modicum of division of labor. It is an illusion to believe in a future society where anyone can engage in or change into any activity he or she wishes, like Marx unfortunately did. This kind of variety and polyvalence is incompatible with excellence and skill. People are finite beings with limited time and abilities.[1] One has to choose one's "trade", try to become skillful and hopefully lead a life of learning and growth, of productive and creative self-development and of self-expression within this "trade". Some changes of heart are of course possible and desirable, but not limitless. But the word "trade" implies division of labor. Communism's hope that automation would reduces the necessity for skills and trades is unrealistic and undesirable as well, given the benefits of excellence (i.e., education, community, belonging, support, etc.). But this division between "trades" is rather different from the highly atomized world of divided labor in industrial processes.

Excellence is not only incompatible with the complete abolition of division of labor. It also requires giving up the demand for total worker equality. The capitalist ideology of managerial expertise is groundless and oppressive.[2] It reduces the workers to executors of the managers' plans. It is obvious that the knowledge necessary to plan is not acquired through theoretical thinking but rather through working practice. So

1 A. MacIntyre, op. cit., p. 197.

2 A. MacIntyre, op. cit., p. 76-106.

the division between workers and managers is artificial and will not hold.

But, on the other hand, complete worker equality will not hold either. Achieving standards of excellence leads, by definition, to differences between people, and it requires dependence (often temporary) on teachers, "masters" and tradition. One can see such a relationship as a form of domination to be combatted, and it certainly is in many capitalist companies where it is often even undone of its original educational aspects. But it doesn't have to be. It can be viewed as transformative for the "pupil". Excellence leads to a good product and to a better producer as well, to someone who can become somebody and who expresses and develops his or her personality through production. This personal transformation through learning and production goes way beyond the transformation of skills. It touches the entire personality.

Communist Politics

Politics according to communism is a kind of fabrication. There is a theory, communism, which functions as a plan, a blueprint for the struggle for a new society, and a blueprint for the new society as such. This plan must be implemented by political means.

The problem with this conception of politics is that it is not democratic. Democratic politics is the struggle between different world views and the reconstruction of society, not according to an indisputable plan, but according to relatively modest proposals of reform of only certain aspects of society, proposals moreover which have only a temporary legitimacy based on majority support and temporary practical success. In a democracy, proposals for reform respect the human rights of all, the economic rights of the poor but at the same time the property rights of the not so poor, or, in case of conflicts between rights, try to find an equitable balance between the rights of all.

In communism, there can be no dispute about the correct political actions, about conceptions of the future of society, or about compromises between different rights. There is a theory and politics must implement it. Full stop. The theory says which goal to pursue and which actions to take in order to pursue it. If the majority disagrees, that's bad luck for the majority. Plurality is destroyed.

If the entire society evolves towards a new form, and if detailed legal reforms of wrongs within the current system are rejected as insufficient or reactionary, even if they improve individual lives dramatically, then all political actions necessary to push this evolution forwards, should encompass the entire society. The society as a whole must be reorganized. A total vision of history implies a total vision of power.

If there is a rationality in history, then power must be given to those who know this rationality best, and it must be absolute power. It is no use letting the people decide who should have power and who should do what with power, because the people with their inferior knowledge cannot judge those with greater knowledge. The latter know better what is good for the rest. When politics is guided by knowledge rather than the struggle between different "knowledges", then popular participation is a nonsense. It seems that communist totalitarianism was not an accident of history and that it is implicit in the theory. The dictatorship of the proletariat, which is in fact shorthand for the dictatorship of the leaders of the proletariat, is the logical conclusion of a certain understanding of politics.

So communism is twice wrong about politics. Its analysis of capitalist politics is, as we have stated, only partly correct and at least one-sided (politics is more than class rule). It does not recognize the enormous possibilities offered by democracy and human rights. It sees the state and the law too much as the products of the economy and disregards the way in which they shape and reshape the economy. And its vision of its own political activity is anti-democratic, violent and tyrannical. Of course, the former has consequences for the latter: if the state has always been an instrument for the oppression of classes, then the communist state can also be oppressive.

> "[I]n view of the fact that during the time of struggle to destroy the old society the proletariat still acts on the foundation of the old society and therefore still gives its movement political forms that more or less belong to the old society, in this time of struggle it has not yet attained its final organization and uses means for its liberation which will fall away after the liberation."[1]

The communist political program, especially the elements of re-education of the remnants of capitalism, forced socialization, and the leadership of the party over an as yet unenlightened proletariat, are quite scary and remind us of the worst parts of the historical communist totalitarian states which, it seems, were not complete aberrations of the original theory.

---

1 K. Marx, Marx Debates Bakunin, in R.C. Tucker, op. cit., p. 547.

Conclusion: The Importance of Work

Communism, it appears, is a highly complex, contradictory and nuanced system of thought, full of things which can still enlighten and help us today, but at the same time marred by shortcomings that can and did have dangerous political consequences. Therefore, a simplistic approach won't do. Outright rejection or adoption isn't possible. The theory has to be modified in such a way that we can reject the errors and excesses and at the same time keep the insights. Such a purified version will allow us to rescue communism from the dustbin of history.

Most of these insights are related to work. The way we work and produce in our capitalist economies is far from satisfactory, even in the most developed ones. The problem of oppression and exploitation, emphasized by communism, is probably no longer the most urgent one in present-day capitalism, at least in its most developed form. But other communist criticisms of capitalism still are, notably the criticism of the way in which capitalism organizes work. Work should be a productive and creative activity, in which we engage, not for the purpose of a wage, survival, prestige, etc., but because it allows us to develop ourselves, be creative, cooperative and masterful.

In our current capitalist system, this ideal is very difficult if not impossible to achieve, for several reasons: the workers have practically no say in the organization or purpose of production because they are hired hands who don't own the means of production; the division of labor makes the whole concept of individual input in production — let alone individual output — a ludicrous notion; and the maximization of profit turns production away from its product and towards an external goal.

However, while the communist diagnosis of the problem of work in capitalism is largely correct and still relevant today, its cure for the disease is not. Communism should adopt a reform approach to capitalism, rather than a revolutionary one. Many reforms have already proven to be very effective, but more are necessary. A revolutionary destruction of capitalism and of the private ownership of the means of production would not only lead to dictatorship and violence, but would also destroy the positive aspects of capitalism (e.g., a relative economic efficiency) and replace them with inferior alternatives (e.g., central planning).

Rather than focusing on the macro level and working towards a New Society, communism should focus on the area where it is best, namely work and productive activity. It is there that communism has the most interesting things to say, and capitalism has the weakest defense.

It is not unreasonable to claim that you are free when you consider your life a work of art, when you constantly try to improve yourself, when you develop your possibilities, when you work on yourself, when you enrich your life and when you try to become what you are potentially. When you can do what you want, unhindered by anyone or anything, you are free in a certain sense of the word, but when you haven't developed yourself and your possibilities, the range of choice for your actions is limited, and hence your freedom is limited, even if no one actually limits your choices. You have limited them yourself because of your lack of self-development.

Communism rightly criticizes capitalism for not allowing people to develop themselves in this way. Freedom understood as self-development is a worthy social goal, but one which needs modifications in the way capitalism organizes work and production. Division of labor and corporate discipline, for example, need to be reformed. We have to destroy the lifetime attachment to detailed production in an opaque and authoritarian system that allows no one to produce in the real sense of the word. Division of labor has to be rebuild. It shouldn't imply pulling people down to the level of human machine appendages in production systems they don't understand. On the contrary, it should push people upward, focusing on excellence and skill as prerequisites for people's self-development. The structures in which we work and produce need to be build again, away from the atomized collections of capitalism or the simple vehicles for revolution promoted by communism, and towards real communities focused on excellence and driven democratically.

REFERENCES

Arendt, H., *Condition de l'homme moderne*, Calmann-Lévy, Paris, 1983

Arendt, H., *La crise de la culture*, Gallimard, Paris, 1992

Arendt, H., *On Revolution*, Penguin Books, Harmondsworth, 1990

Chatelet, F. *Le Capital, Profil d'une oeuvre*, Hatier, Paris, 1975

Eatwell/Milgate/Newman, *Marxian Economics*, W.W. Norton, New York/London, 1990

Ellerman, David, *Marxism as a Capitalist Tool*, http://ssrn.com/abstract=1342814

Engels, F., *Anti-Dühring*, in R.C. Tucker

Engels, F., *Anti-Dühring*, in *Marx-Engels Gesamtausgabe, I, 27*, Dietz Verlag, Berlin, 1988

Engels, F., *Introduction to The Class Struggles in France*, in R.C. Tucker

Engels, F., *Letter to F. Mehring (1893)*, in R.C. Tucker

Engels, F., *Letter to J. Bloch (1890)*, in R.C. Tucker

Engels, F., *Letter to K. Kautsky (1882)*, in R.C. Tucker

Engels, F., *Letter to Th. Cuno*, in R.C. Tucker

Engels, F., *On Authority*, in R.C. Tucker

Engels, F., *On the Division of Labor in Production, Anti-Dühring*, in R.C. Tucker

Engels, F., *Speech at the Graveside of Karl Marx*, in R.C. Tucker

Fukuyama, F., *The End of History and the Last Man*, Penguin Books, Harmondsworth, 1992

Furet, F., *Le passé d'une illusion*, Lafont, Paris, 1995

Geishecker/Goerg, International outsourcing and wages: winners and losers, http://www.etsg.org/ETSG2004/Papers/Geishecker.pdf

Lefort , Cl., *L'invention démocratique*, Fayard, Paris, 1994

Lenin, V. I., *Selected Works vol. 7*

Lenin, V. I., *State and Revolution*, in *Heritage of Western Civilization*, Prentice Hall, New Jersey, 1987

Locke, J. *Second Treatise of Government*, Hackett, Indianapolis, 1980

MacIntyre, A., *After Virtue*, Duckworth, London, 1999

McLellan, D. *Marx*, Fontana Press, London, 1986b

McLellan, D., *The Thought of Karl Marx, Second Edition*, MacMillan, London, Basingstoke, 1986a

K. Marx, *After the Revolution, Marx debates Bakunin*, in R.C. Tucker

Marx, K., *Capital, A Student Edition*, Lawrence & Wishart, London, 1992

Marx, K., *Contribution to the Critique of Hegel's Philosophy of Right*, in R.C. Tucker

Marx, K., *Critique of the Gotha Program*, in R.C. Tucker

Marx, K., *Grundrisse*, in D. McLellan,1986a

Marx, K., *Inaugural Address of the Working Men's International Association*, in R.C. Tucker

Marx, K., *Letter to Engels (1858)*, in R.C. Tucker

Marx, K., *Letter to J. Weydemeyer (1852)*, in R.C. Tucker

Marx, K., *Marx on Bakunin (1875)*, in D. McLellan, 1986a

Marx, K., *Preface to A Contribution to the Critique of Political Economy*, in R.C. Tucker

Marx, K., *Review of E. Girardin, Socialism and Taxes*, in D. McLellan, 1986a

Marx, K., *Speech at the Anniversary of the People's Paper*, in R.C. Tucker

Marx, K., *The Alleged Splits in the International*, in D. McLellan, 1986a

Marx, K., *The German Ideology*, in R.C. Tucker

Marx, K., *The Poverty of Philosophy*, in D. McLellan, 1986a

Marx, K., *The Results of British Rule in India*, in D. McLellan, 1986a

Marx, K., *Theses on Feuerbach*, in R.C. Tucker

Marx, K., *To a conference of the International*, in D. McLellan, 1986b

Marx, K., *Wage Labor and Capital (1849)*, in D. McLellan, 1986a

Marx, Engels, *Address of the Central Committee to the Communist League*, in R.C. Tucker

Marx, Engels, *The Communist Manifesto*, Penguin Books, Harmondsworth, 1985

Marx, Engels, *The Holy Family*, in R.C. Tucker

Paine, T., *The Crisis*, Penguin Books, Harmondsworth, 1995

Popper, K., *The Open Society and its Enemies*, Routledge, London, 1995

Popper, K., *The Poverty of Historicism*, Routledge, London, 1995

Rawls, J. A., *Theory of Justice*, Oxford University Press, Oxford, 1999

Taylor, A. J. P., *Introduction to the Communist Manifesto*, Penguin Books, Harmondsworth, 1985

Tucker, R.C., *The Marx-Engels Reader*, W.W. Norton, New York/London, 1978

Weber, Max, *The Protestant Ethic and the Spirit of Capitalism*, Allen & Unwin, London, 1976

INDEX

A

association, 37, 50, 55-56, 78, 81, 95, 104, 142
automation, 51, 53, 55, 129-132

B

bourgeois, 13, 25-26, 42, 45, 61, 66-67, 70-71, 75, 87, 89-90, 105, 112
bourgeoisie, 9, 14, 22-23, 28, 35, 63, 65, 74, 88, 106, 112-113, 115

C

capitalism, 10, 24, 31, 35, 38, 41-42, 44-47, 55, 63-64, 66, 69-70, 76-78, 81, 83-84, 88, 94, 99, 115, 118, 121-122, 126, 128-129, 131, 135, 137-139, 143
capitalist, 1, 9, 13, 21, 23, 29, 35-37, 39-44, 50-51, 53, 56, 61, 63, 65-71, 75-78, 81, 84, 89, 91, 97, 99, 101, 106-107, 111, 115-116, 127, 129-134, 137-138, 141
capitalists, 13, 24, 34-36, 41, 63-64, 66, 69-70, 74-75, 78, 88-89, 93
China, 10, 83-84
class, 8-10, 12-13, 16-21, 23, 25, 28-29, 34-35, 41-42, 49-50, 61, 63, 65-67, 75-80, 82, 85-86, 88, 93, 102, 104, 106-107, 112, 117, 119, 134, 141
class rule, 8-9, 12-13, 17, 19, 75-77, 82, 106-107, 134
class struggle, 34, 41-42, 66, 75, 77, 85, 88, 119
classless, 43, 77, 111

colonialism, 117

community, 17, 34, 63-66, 94, 99, 104, 111, 113, 132

competition, 10, 23, 41, 53, 63, 66-67, 91-92, 96

consciousness, 13, 15, 17-21, 24-26, 28-29, 31, 64, 68, 71, 79, 84-85, 102-103, 105, 120

contradictions, 9, 42, 105, 121

corporate social responsibility, 123, 125

creative, 43, 47, 49, 51-52, 92, 94, 128, 131-132, 138

crises, 76, 100

crisis, 10, 42, 121, 143

culture, 14, 24, 37, 44, 117-118, 128, 141

D

democracy, 5, 8, 13, 24, 77-78, 86, 88, 92, 96, 98-103, 105-110, 128, 131-133, 135

dependence, 23-24, 35, 41, 43-44, 55, 57, 91-92, 105, 133

determination, 20-21, 84, 102

development, 14-15, 22-23, 26, 28, 32-33, 37, 44-47, 52-53, 55-57, 59-63, 66, 68-70, 73, 77-79, 82-84, 88, 94, 115, 118-120, 127-129

dialectical, 33

dictatorship, 75-78, 82, 85, 125, 134, 138

dictatorship of the proletariat, 75-78, 82, 85, 134

discrimination, 111, 124

division of labor, 36, 41, 51-57, 64, 74, 93, 105, 129-132, 138-139, 142

E

economic rights, 96, 104-105, 107-108, 113, 133

economics, 38, 94-95, 102, 141

economy, 2, 7-9, 15, 22-23, 25-26, 42, 45, 66, 68, 70, 92, 95-96, 102, 105-106, 111, 117-120, 130, 135, 142

education, 18, 24, 80, 106-107, 124, 128, 131-132

egalitarian, 107-108

elections, 101, 107, 109

Engels, Frederich3, 13-15, 25, 28, 34, 36, 45-46, 49-50, 52, 54-55, 57, 63-65, 69, 71, 74-75, 79-80, 85-90, 104-106, 117, 119-120, 141-143

equality, 17-18, 106-112, 132-133

excellence, xi, 77, 97, 130-133, 139

exploitation, 1, 18, 25, 35-36, 43-44, 50, 53, 65, 89, 99, 105-107, 123, 126-127, 137

F

formal, 17-18, 101-102, 105-108

free, 10, 17, 27, 37, 40, 43, 47, 49, 53, 56, 83, 92, 94, 99, 112-113, 116, 121, 124, 128-129, 138-139

freedom, 9, 11-12, 17, 29, 31-32, 34, 42-47, 53, 79, 87-88, 93-94, 96, 108, 110, 112-114, 116, 127-128, 139

H

historical materialism, 84

history, 1, 4-5, 9, 12, 15, 22, 25-26, 28, 31-34, 37, 42-43, 45, 56, 59-63, 67, 73, 79, 81-83,

96, 103, 108, 110, 117-122, 127,
131, 134, 137, 142
human rights, 5, 16-18, 96, 100,
104-118, 123-126, 133, 135

I

ideal, 11, 18-19, 32-33, 42, 49,
68, 100-101, 103, 121, 138
idealism, 42, 84
identity, 29, 48, 52, 112
ideology, 4, 10-13, 17-21, 24, 26,
28-29, 35, 44, 47-48, 54-55,
57, 60-61, 67, 70, 76-77, 101,
132, 143
immiserization, 37, 41, 47
industry, 22, 31, 34, 44, 46-47,
51-52, 61, 66-68, 127
inequality, 17-18, 43, 96, 106-
108, 110-111
inevitable, 9, 31-32, 63-66, 68,
70, 73, 82, 92, 122
influence, 18, 43, 81, 99-103,
105-106, 108-111, 118-119, 123
intensification, 42

K

knowledge, 44-45, 79, 81-83,
107, 131-132, 134

L

labor, 8, 14-15, 18, 21, 23-24, 35-
41, 43-44, 47-58, 61, 63-64,
70-71, 74-75, 82, 91, 93-94,
97-98, 103, 105, 110, 123-127,
129-132, 138-139, 142-143
labor power, 23-24, 35-40, 49-
50, 63, 91, 97-98, 126
law, 8, 10, 13, 15-17, 22, 25, 37,
62-63, 70, 76, 82, 85, 102, 105-
109, 114, 116-117, 120, 126, 135

legal, 15-17, 19-20, 66, 77, 85,
93, 103, 107, 109, 114, 134
legality, 85-88, 103-104
Lenin, Vladimir Ilych 87-89,
142
liberty, 45, 112

M

market, 39, 94, 96, 99, 121, 129
MarKarl, 10, 13, 15, 27, 48, 54,
61, 68, 75, 77-78, 122, 142
material, 15, 18-19, 21-22, 24-
29, 40, 47, 60-62, 68, 70, 81,
83-84, 98, 106-107, 114, 117
maximization, 38, 41-42, 123,
138
means of production, 8, 14-16,
19-20, 22-25, 36-37, 39, 41,
44-45, 47-49, 51, 55-57, 63-
64, 66, 68, 70, 74-77, 81, 85,
88, 91-94, 96, 98-100, 104-
105, 107-108, 128-129, 138
mode of production, 14, 16, 22,
25, 27-29, 56-57, 63, 67-69,
74-75, 81, 118
monopoly, 35
morality, 11, 15, 28, 102, 106

N

natural, 43, 51, 63, 69-70, 82,
123, 127-128
nature, 8, 14, 25, 27-29, 32, 34,
43-47, 51, 57, 60-63, 68, 74,
76, 79, 120, 123, 127-128

O

oppression, 9, 11, 17, 25, 34-36,
42-44, 57, 65, 77-79, 83, 88-
89, 101-102, 114, 127, 135, 137

organization, 9, 13-15, 24, 31, 36, 48, 52-54, 56-57, 67, 71, 75, 79, 84, 92, 96, 98, 100, 102, 130, 135, 138

owner, 53

ownership, 23, 41, 49, 51, 64-65, 75-77, 85-86, 88-89, 91-94, 96, 99-101, 104, 107-108, 121, 138

P

participation, 92-93, 99-100, 103-105, 107, 118, 128, 134

party, 4, 75, 79, 81, 88, 99, 102, 135

philosophy, 12, 15, 67, 78, 122, 142-143

piecemeal, 4, 122

poverty, 23, 33, 42, 44, 47, 50, 67, 73, 78, 82-83, 91, 95, 105, 109, 120, 122, 129, 143

power, 9, 11-13, 16, 18, 22-24, 35-40, 45, 49-50, 53-55, 63, 67, 69, 74-78, 85-87, 91, 97-98, 100-101, 105-112, 114, 123, 126, 128, 134

price, 23, 38-41, 64, 126

private, 1, 10, 13, 16, 34, 49, 51, 57, 63-68, 70-71, 85, 89, 92-94, 96-100, 102-106, 108, 112-115, 121, 127, 131, 138

productivity, 36-38, 44-45, 51, 53-54, 57, 63-65, 129-130

profit, 17, 23, 39-40, 43, 123, 126-128, 138

progress, 9, 25, 31, 46-47, 59, 64, 110, 121-122

proletariat, 8, 21, 28, 36-37, 42, 44, 54, 63-66, 68, 71, 74-80, 82-87, 89, 106, 134-135

property, 5, 10, 13, 16-17, 24-25, 34, 48-49, 57, 63, 66-68, 70-71, 77, 85, 89, 91, 93-94, 96-99, 102, 105-107, 109, 112-114, 116, 128, 131, 133

R

reform, 3, 85, 122, 133, 138

relations of production, 14-15, 20-22, 60-61, 64, 66, 70, 76, 81, 106

religion, 8, 10-12, 15, 28, 34-35, 60, 102-103

reserve army, 36, 92

revolt, 10-12, 42, 65, 69, 78

revolution, 8-9, 20, 22, 26-27, 31, 42, 44-45, 50, 56, 62, 68-71, 75-78, 81-85, 87-89, 104, 107, 115, 122, 139, 141-142

Russia, 83-84

S

scale, 24, 37, 50, 64

science, 2, 31-33, 36-37, 44, 47, 50, 53, 118, 120

self-development, 5, 48, 50-51, 92, 127-128, 132, 139

slavery, 11, 44, 63, 65, 97-98, 118, 124

socialism, 4, 54, 56, 77, 87, 142

socialization, 55-57, 66, 70, 94, 96, 98, 104, 129-130, 135

state, 8, 13, 17, 21, 57, 74-78, 81, 85, 88-89, 95-97, 101, 105, 111, 115-116, 120-121, 128, 135, 142

struggle, 9, 34, 41-42, 44, 46, 66, 75, 77, 85, 87-88, 104, 108-109, 119, 133-135

substructure, 8, 10, 14-16, 19-21, 24, 102

superstructure, 8, 10, 14-16, 19, 102, 119

surplus-value, 36, 38

T

technology, 15, 22, 24, 34, 36, 44, 46, 51, 53, 64, 66, 100, 127, 129-130
theft, 36
thinking, 8, 19, 24-25, 28-29, 89, 103, 111-112, 116-118, 132

U

unequal, 41, 76, 93, 103, 107-108, 112, 120

V

value, 35-42, 47, 49, 57, 63, 93, 96, 98, 113
violations, 105, 123-126
violence, 14, 62, 70, 74, 87-88, 138

W

wage, 15, 35-36, 39, 41, 43, 46, 48-51, 54-57, 61, 68, 93, 123, 126, 128, 138, 143
work, xi, 5, 18-19, 21, 24, 35-37, 39-41, 47-48, 53, 56-57, 60, 80, 85, 91-92, 99, 118-119, 124, 126-132, 137-139
workers, 23-25, 31, 34-38, 41-42, 47-48, 51, 55, 57, 63-64, 66, 74, 76-77, 81, 83, 85-87, 91-93, 97-99, 103-105, 110, 123, 126-133, 138